Canada and the First World War

This book is based on the 50th Anniversary Armistice
Display at the Canadian War Museum, Ottawa. The Canadian
War Museum is part of the National Museum of Man,
National Museums of Canada.

CANADA AND THE

JOHN SWETTENHAM
FIRST WORLD WAR

McGRAW-HILL RYERSON LIMITED
TORONTO, MONTREAL, NEW YORK, LONDON, SYDNEY, JOHANNESBURG, MEXICO, PANAMA, DÜSSELDORF, SINGAPORE, SÃO PAULO, KUALA LUMPUR, NEW DELHI

ISBN 0-07-092978-5
Library of Congress Number 71-84989

1 2 3 4 5 6 7 8 9 10 D-73 1 0 9 8 7 6 5 4 3

Printed and bound in Canada

The illustrations in this book have been reproduced through the courtesy of the Public Archives of Canada and the Photographic Section, National Museums of Canada.

Title page *The 29th Canadian Battalion advancing across No Man's Land during the Battle of Vimy Ridge, April 1917.*

Foreword

The First World War was a tragic episode that stirs us deeply
after more than fifty years. It had great historical significance.
It changed the map of Europe, toppled monarchies,
brought Communist Russia into being, uprooted societies and
destroyed the old days of Victorian certitude forever.
Canada, like many another country, made enormous sacrifices;
she reaped few benefits but what she did are tangible and
remain. The scars of the war, personified by maimed veterans,
are with us still; whole areas of France and Flanders have
been set aside as cemeteries, silent witnesses to what
"The Great War" cost.

In 1967 the Canadian War Museum moved into the old
Archives building on Sussex Drive in Ottawa. These larger
premises gave better facilities for display. The development was
tackled in phases, one of which included the display of
artefacts from World War I. Additionally a special exhibition was
proposed to mark the fiftieth anniversary of the Armistice
which ended World War I. The proposal was supported by other
departments and organizations. In 1968 a committee,
representing the Department of National Defence, the Department
of Veterans Affairs, the Royal Canadian Legion and the
National Gallery, met at the museum to consider what form
the display should take. The Directorate of History of the
Canadian Forces, the Picture Division of the Public Archives and
the Photographic Services of the National Museum were of
tremendous help at a later period. In August the author of
this book, who was familiar with the war and who had written
To Seize the Victory; The Canadian Corps in World War I,
was engaged to write the storyline which was based on
his previous book and other research. Eric Mansfield, a designer
on the museum's staff, set up the display from the written
storyline with all his usual skill.

The exhibition is composed largely of graphics and recaptures
the feeling of the war by use of paintings, contemporary
posters, cartoons and photographs, many never before seen by
the public. Hundreds of photographs were examined. A few,
though well-known, were unique and could not be rejected;
others show us, through unfamiliar eyes, what life, and
even death, in those years was like. The standard of photography

in the First World War was high. We can relive, through photographs, a war of filth and misery; we can see the men who fought it, and the devastated countryside.

The exhibition does more than describe Canada's magnificent contribution by land, sea and air, and the achievements of the men and women who served; it considers the home front and traces the effect of the war on the economy, growth of industry, the impetus given the development of the country by wartime aviation and the effect the war had in bringing about Canada's status as a nation. It was felt important to present the war from all its sides.

The Armistice Display opened at the museum in the presence of more than a hundred veterans drawn from all across the country. Brigadier-General Maurice Watson Harvey, who won the Victoria Cross at the Somme, delivered the opening address. This was the acid test; it was reassuring to know that the exhibition met with the veterans' enthusiastic approval. The display will now tour Canada and be shown in other museums from the fall of 1969 to 1974.

This book is based on the museum's Armistice Exhibition. It combines the storyline with a large number of the illustrations. In this way, it is hoped not only to preserve a significant national display, but to commemorate the sacrifices of the men and women who served so bravely in the war and who fulfilled a national purpose.

Ottawa,
14 April, 1969

L. F. Murray,
Chief Curator
Canadian War Museum

Contents

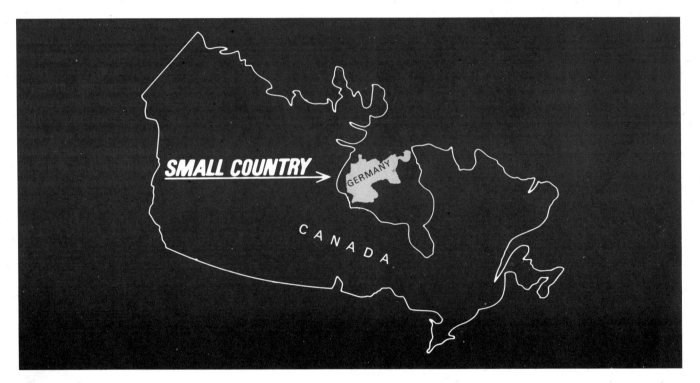

MILITARY PREPAREDNESS 1914

GERMANY		CANADA
65,000,000	POPULATION	7,500,000
856,000	REGULAR ARMY	3,110
8,500,000	MOBILIZED	74,213
79,080	SAILORS	350
29	BATTLESHIPS	0
18	CRUISERS	2
28	SUBMARINES	2
$5,540,000,000	DEFENCE ESTIMATES 1914	$11,000,000

CANADA'S COST 1918

It is estimated that about 10,000 Canadians served in the navy and 24,000 in the air forces; 619,636 Canadian men and women served with the army. Of those in all services 60,661 did not return, roughly ten per cent of all who enlisted. Most of these were soldiers—59,544—as were those who were wounded: 172,950 from the army.

VIII

The Western Front, 1914-1918
CANADIAN OPERATIONS

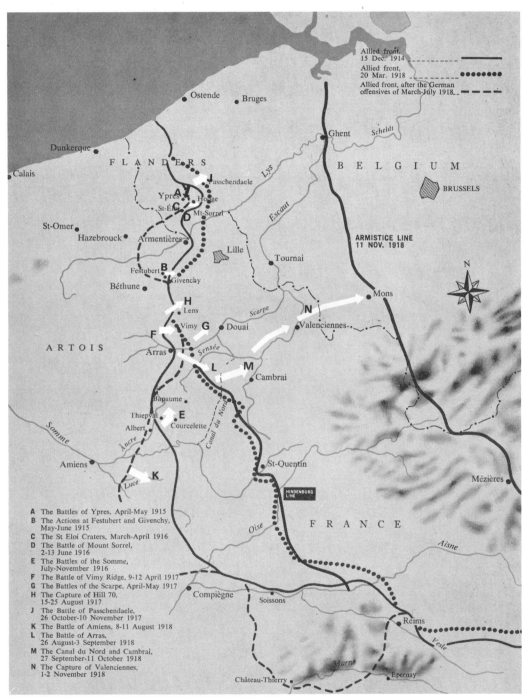

A The Battles of Ypres, April-May 1915
B The Actions at Festubert and Givenchy,
   May-June 1915
C The St Eloi Craters, March-April 1916
D The Battle of Mount Sorrel,
   2-13 June 1916
E The Battles of the Somme,
   July-November 1916
F The Battle of Vimy Ridge, 9-12 April 1917
G The Battles of the Scarpe, April-May 1917
H The Capture of Hill 70,
   15-25 August 1917
J The Battle of Passchendaele,
   26 October-10 November 1917
K The Battle of Amiens, 8-11 August 1918
L The Battle of Arras,
   26 August-3 September 1918
M The Canal du Nord and Cambrai,
   27 September-11 October 1918
N The Capture of Valenciennes,
   1-2 November 1918

Courtesy, The Directorate of History, Canadian Forces Headquarters

Princip Museum, Sarajevo

Gavrilo Princip, the assassin of
Archduke Franz Ferdinand, is
seized at Sarajevo

Part One:
The Call to Arms

Courtesy of the National Gallery of Canada — *Painted by Norman Wilkinson*

CANADA'S ANSWER

The North German Confederation, which expanded to become
the German Empire, and the Canadian Confederation came into
being in the same year—1867. Like other continental powers,
Germany—relatively small in territory but large in population—
built up a large army; Germany also challenged Britain's
supremacy at sea, long unquestioned. Canada, large in territory
and small in population, travelled a different road. The people of
Canada devoted themselves not to military affairs but to
subduing nature and developing the country.

1

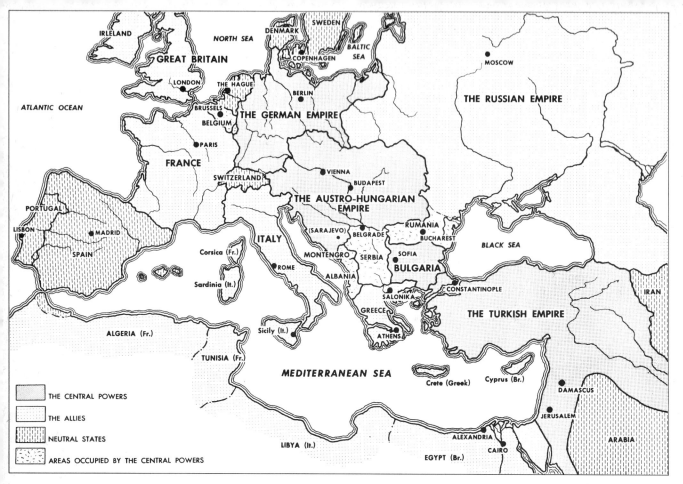

Among the military systems of the continental powers there was a close relation. Each was based on conscription which produced a large reserve by which to expand the active army in time of war. It was in the use of these reserves that the difference lay. Germany, alone, planned to use them from the start in first-line units and thus was able to field a "national" army, supported by the industrial resources of the country, that was much stronger than her opponents had expected.

Britain, counting on her insular position, had only a small regular army; her navy, on the other hand, despite a German challenge in recent years, was still supreme. Like Britain, the Dominions had only small land forces; unlike her, their navies were in their infancy.

The causes of the war are extremely complex and no attempt can be made to describe them here in any detail.

In Canada the summer of 1914 was like every other summer. People enjoyed the sunny days by lakes, rivers and in the woods. Others were by the sea or on the porches of farms and cottages, or of houses in the shady towns. There was little to disturb Canada's easy confidence after a century of peace broken only by minor wars.

Ontario Archives

Summer in the peaceful Ontario town of Wellington,
shortly before the First World War

Shots in Sarajevo caused no echo
in distant Canada

It was known that Europe, through processes which had been developing ever since the Franco-Prussian War, was divided into two armed camps. Germany, Austria-Hungary and Italy were aligned against France and Russia. Britain had no formal alliance with any of these powers but was moving from a policy of isolationism into membership of the European system. No one knew that she had an understanding with France in case of war. Even if they had, it would have caused no alarm. On land, France and Russia were mightier than the Central Powers and the German navy would be no match for the Royal Navy. Shots that rang out in the festive streets of the Balkan town of Sarajevo on 28 June caused no echo in distant Canada.

At Sarajevo, in Bosnia, Gavrilo Princip (who was a member of the Serbian "Black Hand") assassinated Archduke Franz Ferdinand, the visiting heir to the Austro-Hungarian throne. Had he known that his act would ultimately result in more than eight million dead and twenty-one million wounded, his finger might well have hesitated on the trigger. He could not know; the shot was fired, setting alight a powder train that blew up the explosive keg that was Europe.

Serbia and Austria-Hungary, rivals in the Balkans, were eternally at cross-purposes. This time Austria-Hungary would settle with Serbia once and for all. But first, Germany must be

The German Kaiser

sounded out. Would Germany support Austria in this?
Germany would, and on 5 July counselled Austria to take strong
action against Serbia. Germany, moreover, would continue
to support Austria even if Russia came to the help of Serbia.
There was no conscious determination on Germany's part to
plunge Europe into war. Germany's answer was an instrument
of bluff and threat such as had been successfully employed
often before. But this time the threat miscarried. The German
Kaiser's "blank cheque" to Austria stands out predominantly
among the immediate causes of the war.

On 23 July, armed with this cheque, the Austro-Hungarian
Government served an ultimatum on Serbia with terms so harsh
that Serbia could hardly accept them. Serbia, however, did so
with the exception of just enough to save her from complete
humiliation. In these reservations Austria found sufficient cause
to go to war, which she declared on 26 July. Serbia appealed
to Russia, the self-proclaimed protector of the Slav nations
in the Balkans, and Russia had her own motive for not wishing
to see Serbia overcome. If Germany and Austria-Hungary
smashed Serbia they would dominate the Balkans—and hence
Constantinople and the Bosphorus through which the bulk of
Russia's trade with the outside world passed. Russia, with
good reason, could not allow hostile hands to crush her
windpipe. She sought—again a threat—to curb Austria-Hungary
by mobilizing, ordered on 30 July.

Germany viewed Russia's mobilization with alarm. Germany's
strategy in case of war was governed by the "Schlieffen Plan,"
the brainchild of Graf Schlieffen, Chief of the German General
Staff from 1891 to 1905. Working on the assumption that
war would be fought on two fronts against the French and
Russian armies, Schlieffen conceived a plan for a speedy
decision against the French while the Russians, whose
mobilization was proverbially slow, were being held in check.
Only ten divisions were allowed for use against the Russians.
The mass of the German forces were to be concentrated against
the French. Nearly three-quarters of the German Army were to
mass on a heavy right wing for a wheel through Holland
and Belgium (modified later by Schlieffen's successor,
von Moltke, to omit Holland), through northern France, across
the Seine west of, and thus enclosing, Paris. This wing was

A British view of the German invasion of Belgium

then to drive southeast to press the French back against
Switzerland and the German defences in Lorraine; there,
squeezed in an iron grip, the hapless French would be
annihilated. Only then, with the western front secure, would
the Germans concentrate against Russia. The Russian decision
to mobilize threatened to throw the Schlieffen Plan out of gear;
unless mobilization were checked, the Germans might lose
the advantage of speed, based on an efficient railway system,
on which they counted; they might be faced with a war on
two fronts after all. Germany, therefore, sent an ultimatum
demanding that the Russians demobilize within twelve hours.
Russia refused. On 1 August, Germany declared war on Russia.
Two days later, with the thinnest of pretexts, Germany also
declared war on France. Italy, claiming that she was committed
only in a defensive war, elected to be neutral. Britain wavered,
but mobilized the fleet. Then Germany, moving against France,
invaded Belgium whose neutrality was guaranteed by
Britain (as well as Germany). Britain's ultimatum to Germany to
withdraw her troops from Belgium brought no reply and on
4 August Britain too was in the struggle.

German troops, on the way to Belgium, leave Berlin

WEATHER FORECASTS

Victoria and Vicinity—Fresh to strong winds, mostly westerly and southerly, generally fair.
Lower Mainland—Light to moderate winds, generally fair, not much change in temperature.

The Daily Colonist.

(ESTABLISHED 1858)

COLONIST TELEPHONES

Business Office 11
Circulation 11
Job Printing 197
Editorial Rooms 50

O. 202--FIFTY-SIXTH YEAR | VICTORIA, VANCOUVER ISLAND, BRITISH COLUMBIA, WEDNESDAY, AUGUST 5, 1914 | FOURTEEN PAGES

British Empire Has Declared War Against Germany

KING GEORGE V

H.M.S. IRON DUKE, THE LATEST ADDITION TO THE IMPERIAL NAVY

LEETS TO MEET IN NORTH SEA

eatest Naval Battle in World's History May Soon Be Fought—British Destroyer Chased by Cruiser.

ELGIUM FIGHTS FOR INDEPENDENCE

ndon Crowd Makes Attack on German Embassy—French President and Premier Make Statements.

...—Great Britain declared war on Germany tonight. The ... of the British ... the whole world ... before the expiration of the time set by Great ... to Germany ... a satisfactory reply on the ... of Belgian neutrality. Germany's reply was a summary ... of the request that Belgian neutrality should be respected.

The British Ambassador at Berlin ... received his passports and ... British Government notified Germany that a state of war existed between the two countries.

Countries in Strife

... of Europe is now in arms. Austria-Hungary and Germany are opposed ... Russia, France and Great Britain, Servia and Montenegro.

Italy has declared her neutrality, but ... mobilizing. Belgium, Holland and ... have mobilized. The German demand that the Belgian Government shall permit the free passage of German troops through Belgium was ... by hasty preparations to resist such an advance across Belgian territory. Sweden has made no answer to ... from Russia and Germany regarding her attitude, but is preparing to defend her neutrality.

... is making ready to live up to ... alliance with Great Britain in case ... certain eventualities.

... is reported to be preparing a proclamation of neutrality.

Austria-Hungary for the moment has ... from her campaign against Servia ... the purpose of holding back ... and Servia has mobilized with ... avowed intention of invading Bosnia.

Pressure on Belgium

BRUSSELS, Aug. 4.—Germany in her ... to Belgium declared that if Belgium adopted a hostile attitude against German troops and put difficulties ... the way of their advance, Germany would be obliged to consider Belgium an enemy. In that case Germany would ... enter into any undertaking with Belgium, but would leave final relations of the two states to the decision of arms."

Fleets in Open Sea

LONDON, Aug. 3.—The King held a ... council sitting just before midnight. A decree had been prepared, ... that a state of war existed with Germany, should the reply to England's ultimatum prove unsatisfactory. Instead the Kaiser ignored the ultimatum. England must strike on the sea in ... to prevent any invasion of its ... by Germany.

The German battle fleet is sweeping ... North Sea. It was admitted by the Admiralty last night that a British destroyer, which located the Germans late yesterday, was chased by a German ... cruiser, but managed to escape. ... were exchanged, but no damage was done.

The worst demonstration so far took ... last night when an enormous mob ... the German embassy. Stones ... thrown through the windows and ... was checked by the arrival of ... police. The officers had to charge ... crowd repeatedly before it could be ... The attack was renewed, ... mounted officers rode down the ... of the mob. Troops have been ... to defend the embassy.

Fight at Liege

BRUSSELS, Aug. 4.—It is reported ... that following a demand by the Germans for the surrender of the city ... Liege an engagement ensued in ... the Germans were repulsed. All Germans have been expelled from Liege ... Namur.

Germany's Treachery

PARIS, Aug. 4.—President Poincare ... address to the Senate and Chamber ... declared that Germany "had ... treacherously towards France," ... "France is vigilant as well ... She was ready, and our ...

Continued on Page 11, Col. 2

FINAL PEACE EFFORT

Messages Exchanged by King George and Emperor of Russia on Eve of War

LONDON, Aug. 4.—King George's ... to the Russian Emperor in a ... effort to avoid war and the Emperor's reply have been made public. ... King, expressing the opinion that ... had been some misunderstanding ... to the breaking off of the negotiations, said:

"I make a personal appeal to you to ... the misapprehension and leave ... ground for negotiations for ... peace."

The Russian Emperor replied that he ... have accepted the proposals had ... Germany declared war.

"Germany," said the Emperor, "showed ... disposition to mediate and her preparations and those of Austria made it ... that Russia should mobilize. ... I gave most categorical assurances ... German Emperor that the Russian troops would not move so long as ... negotiations continued."

The reply concludes:

"I trust that your country will not ... to support Russia and France. God ... and protect you."

CANADIANS ARE READY TO SERVE

News of Declaration of War Causes Demonstrations of Patriotism in Cities—Thousands of Men Volunteer.

QUEBEC, Aug. 4.—The announcement that Germany and Great Britain were at war was received here with the greatest enthusiasm, while English French and Irish paraded together in a display of loyalty and patriotism such as has never before been witnessed in the ancient capital.

Before a great crowd, Albert Sevigny, the brilliant young Member of Parliament for Dorchester, made it plain that the French Canadians realized the seriousness of the present menace to the Empire in general and Canada in particular, and were standing with their fellow citizens. He recalled how France had gone down before the arms of Germany in 1870. The great question which French Canadians had been asking during the past few days, he said, had been "what will Britain do?"

Had France been left alone, her arms might not have met with success, but she would receive the happy news that the entente cordiale was no idle word. England has arisen to the occasion. Whatever the results might be they would go into war with a united front, and he was sure that Providence would smile upon them in this struggle.

London Enthusiastic

LONDON, Ont., Aug. 4.—Public enthusiasm ran high in the city tonight when the news was announced that war had been declared between Great Britain and Germany.

At the Capital

OTTAWA, Aug. 4.—Not since the memorable South African war have such scenes of patriotism been witnessed in the Capital as tonight, when the news of the declaration of war was received. Thousands stood in the streets and sang the national anthem, "The Maple Leaf Forever," and "O Canada." The Canadian Cabinet was in session almost conspicuously, with the Duke of Connaught in close touch with his advisers. The staff of the Militia Department has been on duty ever since the crisis.

Toronto Aroused

TORONTO, Aug. 4.—Although a state of war between Germany and Great Britain had been expected, the official declaration came with a shock. Immense crowds gathered at the newspaper offices waiting for definite news. When finally the bulletins were posted placing the matter beyond doubt and the intelligence was disseminated, it was at first received in silence. Then all possible consequences were forgotten in an outburst of patriotism and the streets resounded with cheers for the Empire.

Never since the memorable Pretoria night has this city witnessed such a spontaneous outburst of patriotism and whole-souled loyalty to the Empire. All night bands paraded the streets at the head of crowds waving flags and cheering for the King and country.

The crowds sang patriotic songs. Intense interest prevailed at military

Continued on Page 2, Col. 2

BRITAIN'S FLEET GOES INTO ACTION

LONDON, Aug. 4.—Britain's wireless broke loose tonight. Immediately after midnight King George sent a special message to the British fleet sailing against the German armada, cleared for action.

"I have confidence that the British fleet will revive the old glories of the navy. I am sure that the navy will again shield Britain in this hour of trial. It will prove the bulwark of the Empire."

This was the first message sent to the fleet since it cleared from Plymouth Harbor and sailed to the secret rendezvous in the North Sea. Ever since then the wireless had been silent. No word was permitted to go forth, until tonight the signal for the most tremendous naval battle ever fought flashed out through the darkness from the great naval wireless station.

Immediately after the order to capture or destroy the enemy had been flashed to the Admiral commanding, it was followed by the King's own words.

READY RESPONSE TO EMPIRE'S CALL

Sir Richard McBride Convinced That British Columbians Stand Ready to Prove Worthy of Traditions of Race.

Sir Richard McBride, when asked for an expression of opinion on the receipt of the declaration of war between Great Britain and Germany last evening, made a statement on behalf of British Columbia as follows:

"British Columbia receives the news of the declaration of war with Germany with that quiet and studied determination to stand by the Empire with all her might that has characterized the action of this section of His Majesty's Dominions since its earliest settlement. As one of the outposts of the Empire, it is quite possible that a great deal of interest will focus on this point, and I am sure that the fact that within the last few hours there has been a tremendous outburst of loyalty from the

Continued on Page 13, Col. 5

BRITISH VESSEL SUNK BY GERMANS

LONDON, Aug. 5.—A British mine-laying ship has been sunk by a German fleet.

The British torpedo boat destroyer Pathfinder was pursued by the fleet, but managed to make her escape.

IMPOSING PROCESSION

Jews in Paris Demonstrate Their Readiness to Support France in Great Contest

PARIS, Aug. 4.—One of the most imposing patriotic processions in Paris yesterday was formed by more than 2,000 Jews, who responded to the call of the Hebrew Association of Paris to join in the manifestations supporting the country.

Jews of all nationalities friendly to France marched through the principal streets, headed by a great banner, upon which were the words, "Jews, come to the aid of France."

English, French, Russian and Belgian flags were carried in the procession, which wended its way along the streets, singing the "Marseillaise", heartily cheered by the populace.

HOLD SESSION OF PARLIAMENT

Cabinet Decides to Issue Summons to Members to Meet Tuesday, August 18—Military Measures Necessary.

OTTAWA, Aug 4—At the conclusion of tonight's Cabinet council meeting, the Premier announced that Parliament would be summoned on Tuesday, August 18. The first business of Parliament will be to vote the funds required for defence purposes and to ratify the Governor-General's warrants which have already been issued. There will be legislation necessary to legalise action which has already been taken by the Militia Department under authority from the Cabinet, exceeding some of the powers granted by the Militia Act. These ... for emergency actions in requisitioning troops for special purposes, and in expending money for which there was no parliamentary vote.

Continued on Page 13, Col. 5

FRENCH ARMY CROSSES BORDER

Invades Germany by Way of Alsatian Frontier—Column Is Said to Number 75,000 Men.

BERLIN, Aug. 4.—A French army is invading Germany by way of Alt Muensterol, on the Alsatian border ten miles east of Belfort, according to official information given out by the German war office last night. The German border patrols are resisting the advance of the French column, which numbers 75,000 men, but the patrol is retiring gradually in face of the superior numbers.

The German army corps are on the way to meet the invasion. According to the German official, the French force is supported by heavy artillery, and is accompanied by a detachment of army aviators, who have been flying across the border in reconnoitering flights. There also is a motor cycle scouting detachment, which crossed the border ahead of the main column, according to these reports.

The present Russian operations of the German army are confined to three army corps, but 500,000 reservists will be added to this force as soon as they can be moved to the border. German frontier guards have forced back Russian patrols at Richenreid and Tiloslav after brief skirmishing, according to reports received in Berlin.

Continued on Page 13, Col. 5

GREAT BRITAIN DECLARES WAR

Action Taken Following Germany's Rejection of Request That Neutrality of Belgium Be Respected.

FLEET AND ARMY ARE WELL PREPARED

Premier Asquith's Statement in House of Commons—Three Ministers Retiring From the Government.

LONDON, Aug. 4.—Britain declared war against Germany tonight. This announcement was made at the Foreign Office after midnight. England is ready. Orders have already been sent to the commander-in-chief of the British naval forces to wipe out the German fleet. It is believed that if the fleet has not already struck it will do so in the next few hours.

Foreign Office Statement

The British Foreign Office has issued the following statement:

"Owing to the summary rejection by Germany of the request made by His Britannic Majesty's Government, that the neutrality of Belgium should be respected, His Majesty's Ambassador at Berlin has received his passports, and His Majesty's Government has declared to the German Government that a state of war exists between Great Britain and Germany from 11 o'clock p. m., August 4."

Vice-Admiral Sir John Jellicoe today assumed supreme command of the British home fleet, with the acting rank of Admiral. His chief of staff will be Rear-Admiral Charles E. Madden.

Funds for Defence

BRUSSELS, Aug. 4.—The Chamber passed a bill appropriating $10,000,000 for purposes of defence.

Belgian Town Taken

LONDON, Aug. 4.—A dispatch to the Central News Agency from Amsterdam says the Germans have captured Vise, Belgium, a town with a population of 3,000, situated on the River Meuse, eight miles from Liege.

German Ships Seized

BORDEAUX, France, Aug. 4.—Two German ships in this port have been seized.

Premier's Statement

LONDON, Aug. 4.—Mr. Asquith speaking in Parliament today said: We have received from the Belgian legation here the following telegram from the Belgian Minister of Foreign Affairs:

"'The Belgian general staff announces that Belgian territory has been violated at Verviers, near Aix La Chapele.'

"Subsequent information tends to show that a German force has penetrated still further into Belgian territory.

"We also received" this note this morning from the German Ambassador here: "'Please dispel any distrust that may subsist on the part of the British Government with regard to our intentions by repeating most positively the formal assurance that even in case of armed conflict with Belgium, Germany will, under no pretensions whatever, annex Belgian territory.

"'The sincerity of this declaration is borne out by the fact that we have solemnly pledged our word to Holland strictly to respect her neutrality. It is obvious that we could not profitably annex Belgian territory without making territorial acquisition at the expense of Holland.

"'Please impress on Sir Edward Grey that the German army could not remain exposed to a French attack across Belgium which was planned according to absolutely unimpeachable information. Germany has as a consequence disregarded Belgian neutrality to prevent what means to her a question of life and death—a French advance through Belgium.'"

Continued on Page 11, Col. 1

FOOD PRICES ADVANCE

Flour Raised Fifty Cents Per Barrel at Toronto—Other Commodities Dearer in Proportion

TORONTO, Aug. 4.—Flour advanced 50 cents per barrel today as a result of the war situation. Sugar advanced 10 cents yesterday, and another advance is expected at any moment. It is now $4.61 per cwt. Canned meats of all kinds that have not been sold ahead will be increased in price. This also applies to canned vegetables and fruit.

Wholesale grain merchants see in the crop conditions in the West justification for wheat at $1.10 to $1.15 a bushel. They add to this the possibilities of war conditions and evolve a price for products that may be startling.

In view of the large wheat supply to Britain as the result of the present crisis, preparations will likely be made for the placing of day and night crews in all the elevators along the shipping points of the Great Lakes. This action will be taken by the dock owners to avoid delaying shipping.

FIFTY YEARS AGO TODAY

(From The Colonist of August 5, 1864)

Turn Verein—The Turn Verein of this city held their opening ball last evening in the Lyceum Hall. His Excellency Governor Kennedy was in attendance and about 150 other guests including many officers of the Navy.

Since the miners have started prospecting at Sooke, there have been granted twelve licenses for the Sooke Mining District, for selling spirits.

Short of Hands—We understand that the steamer Thames is short of hands, and other steamers in port are also feeling the effect of the gold excitement caused by the news brought to town in the last forty-eight hours. We think that it will be the means of taking many passengers from the mail boat which is to sail today for New Westminster, if not her crew. The Chinamen are now working claims on the Leach River and there is a strong disposition amongst the miners to oust them from the workings. Gold is now selling at $20 per ounce.

Le Devoir

VOLUME V—No 286

MONTREAL, LUNDI 3 AOUT, 1914

UN SOU LE NUMERO

ABONNEMENTS :

Edition Quotidienne :
CANADA ET ETATS-UNIS $3.00
UNION POSTALE $8.00

Edition Hebdomadaire :
CANADA $1.00
ETATS-UNIS $1.50
UNION POSTALE $2.00

Rédaction et Administration :
43 RUE SAINT-VINCENT
MONTREAL

TELEPHONES :
ADMINISTRATION : Main 7461
RÉDACTION : Main 7460

LE DEVOIR

Directeur : HENRI BOURASSA

FAIS CE QUE DOIS !

L'ANGLETERRE MOBILISERA DEMAIN

LA GUERRE

Encore qu'il faille prendre chacune des dépêches avec beaucoup de précautions — elles se contredisent souvent l'une l'autre — il semble bien que le monde marche à une catastrophe incommensurable, suivant l'expression de M. Asquith.

Aucune époque n'a vu une guerre dont les conséquences s'annoncent aussi graves que celle d'aujourd'hui. C'est la première fois qu'un conflit de proportions aussi considérables s'engage sous le régime de la *nation armée*, c'est la première fois que des armes nouvelles comme l'aéroplane et le sous-marin seront employées sur une aussi vaste échelle. Et les liens intimes créés entre tous les peuples par les moyens modernes de communication font que toutes les nations, même celles qui ne seront pas directement intéressées, ressentiront, dans une proportion qu'on ne peut encore apprécier, le contrecoup du conflit.

Songe qu'en vertu des lois militaires des grandes nations déjà engagées, tous les hommes valides de vingt à quarante-cinq ans — sans compter les officiers plus âgés — seront appelés sous les armes. C'est dire qu'en dehors de la perturbation causée par la guerre elle-même — de la saisie et de l'emploi par les gouvernements des chemins de fer, des télégraphes, des téléphones et de tous les grands moyens de transport, de l'énorme gaspillage financier qu'entraînera le conflit — nous allons [...] à une suspension quasi-complète de la production sur une par[...]

BILLET DU SOIR.

prix, si incertain quant aux travaux, en général, si peu satisfaisant, que après un an d'expérience, on s'est vu obligé, d'abord de le supplémenter de contrats partiels, et finalement de le supprimer.

Le premier résultat de cette politique est de retarder inutilement les travaux, d'ennuyer la population appelée à contribuer au coût de construction de cette route et de mécontenter beaucoup de contribuables.

On a dit que le coût si élevé de construction du Boulevard Edouard VII était dû en partie à la température défavorable durant la construction.

On ne pourra toujours pas invoquer cette raison pour la route Edouard VII. On pourrait difficilement demander deux étés plus favorables que ceux de 1913 et 1914.

J. D.

LA FRANCE VICTORIEUSE A LA FRONTIERE
COMBAT NAVAL DANS LA MER DU NORD

LA RUSSIE ENVAHIE

BERLIN, 3. — L'invasion de la Russie par les troupes allemandes a commencé aujourd'hui, par l'occupation de Kalisz, situé dans la Pologne Russe. Le premier bataillon du cent cinquantième régiment d'infanterie et une compagnie d'artillerie se sont emparés de la ville.

LA DOUARIERE RUSSE ARRETEE A BERLIN

Londres, 3. — L'impératrice douairière de Russie, Marie Feodorowna, la sœur de la reine mère Alexandra, a vu mettre un terme à son voyage à Berlin. On lui a donné le choix de retourner en Angleterre, ou d'aller à Copenhague.

LA FRANCE EN ETAT DE SIEGE

Paris, 3. — Le décret établissant la loi martiale a été promulgué d'un [...]

AVEC LA FRANCE

D'après une déclaration de Sir Edward Grey, l'Angleterre se serait engagée à défendre la France, au cas où un navire de guerre allemand attaquerait ses côtes sur la Manche.

Mme MESSIMY AMBULANCIERE

Paris, 3.— Mme Messimy, la femme du ministre de la guerre, a organisé un corps d'ambulancières de la Croix Rouge.

UN TRUC QUI ECHOUE

Coblenz, Allemagne, 3.— Quatre-vingt officiers français portant l'uniforme prussien ont tenté, hier, par [...]

"Empire du Kaiser, c'est-à-dire le Danemark."

LES SOCIALISTES RUSSES

Londres, 3.— Le correspondant du "Morning Post" à Saint-Pétersbourg dit que les socialistes sont en faveur de la guerre. Les personnes riches offrent leurs villas d'été aux autorités militaires pour qu'elles soient transformées en hôpitaux.

The Globe

THE MARKETS
Canadian, New York, and London closed.
[...] October wheat closed 2½c higher

VOLUME LXXI.

TORONTO, WEDNESDAY, AUGUST 5, 1914—SIXTEEN PAGES.

NUMBER 20,138.

THE WEATHER.
Probabilities :—Fair and warmer ; thunder-showers at night.
The sun rises at 5.16 a.m. and sets at 7.57 p.m.
Next British mail, via the Empress of Britain, from Quebec, closes to-day at 6 p.m.

GREAT BRITAIN AND GERMANY ARE NOW AT WAR

LONDON, Aug. 4.—The British Foreign Office has issued the following statement :—"Owing to the summary rejection by the German Government of the request made by his Britannic Majesty's Government that the neutrality of Belgium should be respected, his Majesty's Ambassador at Berlin has received his passports, and his Majesty's Government has declared to the German Government that a state of war exists between Great Britain and Germany from 11 o'clock p.m., August 4."

THE BULWARK OF BRITAIN'S EMPIRE GOES FORTH AGAIN TO BATTLE

King George Says the Navy Will Revive Its Glories in Action

A Dramatic Scene as the King and the Statesmen of Britain Waited the Striking of the Clock, Which Meant War—Stirring Message to the Fleet Was the First Sign That Has [...]

MR. ASQUITH'S STORY OF THE ULTIMATUM

Germany's Amazing View of Neutrality Agreement

Billions Voted

(Canadian Press Despatch.)
London, Aug. 4.—The House of Commons voted $525,000,000 for emergency purposes, and passed several bills in the minutes without a dissenting vote to-day.

(Canadian Press Despatch.)
Berlin, Aug. 4.—A bill was introduced into the German Imperial Parliament to-day providing [...]

Britain Could Not Accept It in Any Way as Satisfactory, Said the Premier, and Therefore Sent an Ultimatum to Germany.

WAR SUMMARY

IT IS WAR. Diplomacy has said the last word, and the diplomats have separated wrangling—even after their taxis had been ordered—as to who was really to blame. The sword must now settle the controversy. It will be a terrific struggle waged all over the world. Into the vortex have already been drawn Germany and Austria on the one hand, and Servia, Russia, France, Belgium and Great Britain on the other. Italy and Turkey may yet join Germany and Austria, and Holland will probably take a part with the Belgians and their allies in seeking to safeguard the independence of the Low Countries against German aggression. . . . . .

PARLIAMENT CALLED FOR AUGUST 18TH

Army Division of 23,000 to be Mobilized

PROTECTING VITAL POINTS

Armed Forces Guarding Ports and Cable and Wireless Stations—Will Protect Canals and Other Means of Transportation and Communication

The Canadian Parliament [...]

The Morning Chronicle

"Nova Scotia's Greatest Paper."

CITY EDITION
WAR SPECIAL

VOL. LII. NO. 193

HALIFAX NOVA SCOTIA WEDNESDAY AUGUST 5 1914

TEN PAGES.

PRICE TWO CENTS

BRITAIN STRIKES; THE NAVY SAILS TO SINK ENEMY

GERMAN FLEET STRUCK BEFORE WAR DECLARED

BRITAIN'S DECLARATION OF WAR

LONDON, August 4.--The British Foreign Office has issued the following statement :

"Owing to the summary rejection by the German Government of the request made by His Britannic Majesty's Government that the neutrality of Belgium should be respected, His Majesty's Ambassador at Berlin has received his passports, and His Majesty's Government has declared to the German Government that a state of war [...]

BRITAIN CALLED KAISER'S BLUFF FORCING ISSUE

In 1914, unlike today, when Britain was at war Canada was at war. But there was no reluctance as both Sir Robert Borden (the Prime Minister) and Sir Wilfrid Laurier (the Leader of the Opposition) made clear. On the contrary, the enthusiasm which had swept the London crowds at the expiry of Britain's ultimatum was matched in Canada. Believing that Britain's cause was just, men eagerly streamed in to join the colours; their main fear was that the war would be over before they could take part.

Canada, apart from enthusiastic men, had little with which to help oppose the German might. The strength of the Permanent Force was only about 3,000. It is true that the forces had improved since the end of the South African War; since 1900 the militia had been slowly modernized. New armouries, rifle

Sir Robert Borden, Canada's wartime Prime Minister

Eager recruits, Ottawa

ranges, a large camp at Petawawa, and even a tiny general staff, had been put in hand by Sir Frederick Borden, the Defence Minister in the Liberal administration. The militia establishment had increased from some 35,000 in 1901 to 66,000 by 1914 and the 25,000 who attended training camps in 1904 had become 55,000 in 1913; but this was feeble by European standards. Energetic Colonel Sam Hughes, who succeeded Borden as Minister of Militia and Defence in 1911, had secured larger defence funds while in office — $7 million in 1911 had become $11 million by 1914. Hughes brought a new excitement and impetus to military reform. He had continued a divisional

Sir Wilfrid Laurier, leader of the Opposition

Colonel Sam Hughes

Men of the 11th Battalion, Valcartier

PATRIOTIC DEMONSTRATION OF UNPARALLELED FERVOR CALLED FORTH BY GERMANY'S CHALLENGE

REGINA GOES FIGHTING MAD WHEN RUPTURE BETWEEN GREAT BRITAIN AND GERMANY IS ANNOUNCED——THREE THOUSAND PERSONS DEMONSTRATE IN FRONT OF LEADER OFFICE AND ON STREETS OF CITY, SINGING TO ACCOMPANIMENT OF BOY SCOUTS' BAND—STIRRING SCENES—MEN BREAK FROM PROCESSIONS TO ENROL THEIR NAMES AMONG VOLUNTEERS.

Canada's peacetime soldiers

system of organization for the militia, which was useful for it was in these formations that the men would fight. Not only that; he accelerated the work of his predecessor in the provision of armouries, improved rifle ranges, and the procurement of better weapons. Canadians even manufactured their own service rifle— the Ross. This might have been a sound step if the rifle had been reliable. In fact the Ross rifle, joint brainchild of Hughes and Borden, was defective and Hughes' praise and retention of the Ross, despite evidence of its faults, was to embitter the troops who had to use it. The most that can be said of the militia, despite the energy of Colonel Hughes, is that Canada had a nucleus ground force on which to build when war broke out.

There was little strength by sea and none by air. Since 1910 Canada had had a navy of two cruisers, H.M.C.S. *Niobe* and H.M.C.S. *Rainbow*, purchased from the Admiralty as training ships. Not much could be expected from them in 1914. *Niobe* lay at Halifax, unfit for sea duty for many weeks, and in any case the whole naval manpower consisted of fewer than 350 officers and men—less than half the number required to man her. The smaller vessel, *Rainbow*, could be manned and put to sea but she was not ready for operations. There was no air branch in the Canadian forces.

Recruits in Montreal

Troops leave Toronto for Valcartier

Canada had a mobilization plan for war. This would transfer the six divisions of the militia to a war footing as far as their incomplete organization and deficiencies might permit. It would also mobilize for active service overseas a Canadian contingent of a division and a mounted brigade. Canada's offer of this overseas contingent was gratefully accepted by Britain but Hughes scrapped the mobilization plan so far as the infantry was concerned. He substituted for its orderly procedures a personal "call to arms" and a concentration at Valcartier where no camp as yet existed. He did not mobilize the units of the militia; instead, he raised new battalions which were known by number and thus did not perpetuate traditional and honoured names. One new battalion, however, had a name—Princess Patricia's Canadian Light Infantry. This unit, raised and largely equipped by Hamilton Gault of Montreal, consisted of veterans and preceded the others overseas. Battalions had to be formed, clothing and equipment issued; men had to be medically examined amidst the turmoil of construction while the paraphernalia of war (much of which proved unserviceable) arrived by the cartload at Valcartier. The result was chaos. The artillery, on the other hand, mobilized according to plan and without hysteria.

Canadian gunners at Valcartier

The 24th Battalion marches through the streets of Montreal before going overseas

"Canada's Great Armada" painted by Frederick S. Challener

Colonel Hughes promised 25,000 men. Such was the response that by 8 September 32,665 officers and men had assembled in the tented camp and these, formed into provisional brigades but still untrained, embarked at Quebec and on 3 October began the Atlantic crossing in thirty ships. Another ship carried the 2nd Lincolns which the Royal Canadian Regiment had relieved in Bermuda. A thirty-second ship, with the Newfoundland Contingent, joined the convoy at sea. Thirty-two ocean liners, closely escorted by four British light cruisers and protected by battleships farther out, made the crossing safely and arrived at Plymouth after a twelve-day voyage. Here was "Canada's answer" and the British cheered.

"Canada sends her aid at a timely moment." (Winston Churchill, First Lord of the Admiralty)

Lieutenant-General E. A. H. Alderson

Canadian troops on Salisbury Plain

The Canadians were not yet trained or equipped for battle. They were fitted out and exercised on Salisbury Plain during the wettest winter in living memory. Formed into the Canadian Division under Lieutenant-General E. A. H. Alderson, a British officer, they were deemed ready for France by the end of January, 1915. On 4 February King George V and Field-Marshal Lord Kitchener (the British War Minister) reviewed them in pouring rain. Sodden flags and pennants drooped heavily against their staves but the men were smart and steady. A few days later they embarked for France.

The Newfoundland Contingent remained in England. Formed into the Newfoundland Regiment, it fought with the British throughout the war. The Patricia's had already joined the British in France. The cavalry units, formed into the Canadian Cavalry Brigade under Colonel J. E. B. Seely (another British officer), also remained for the time in England as did Canadian machine-gun units.

Salisbury Plain—a contemporary cartoon

Salisbury Plain: the floods were too much for motor transport

Leaving Salisbury Plain for the Western Front

At the beginning of the war the Germans had more machine-guns than the Allies

18

Part Two:
1915, First Fighting:
for the 1st Division

Courtesy of the National Gallery of Canada   *—Painted by Richard Jack*

THE SECOND BATTLE OF YPRES

On 16 February, after butting Biscayan rollers for four days, the 1st Division completed disembarkation at St. Nazaire where it was warmly welcomed by the French. There the troops entrained in box-cars for the level plains of Flanders. After the miseries of Salisbury Plain they were sure that the worst of their troubles were over.

By the time the Canadians arrived in France the Western Front, offering no flank that could be turned, stretched in a continuous line from the North Sea to neutral Switzerland. Enemy and Allied trenches, sandbagged and defensively wired, faced each other across the shell-torn ground of no-man's-land.

They came in February, 1915, for a week's indoctrination with British units holding the line in front of Armentières. Every man, from company commander down to private, spent forty-eight

19

"Landing of the First Canadian Division at Saint Nazaire"   *Painted by Edgar Bundy*

hours with his opposite number for individual training—a
thorough introduction to the mysteries of trench warfare.
That was followed by twenty-four hours of platoon training,
during which the Canadian platoons took over the responsibility
for a definite length of trench. The men—eager, doubtful, and
afraid—marched up from their billets along the glistening
pavé roads. They passed smashed and broken farmhouses and
cottages, stunted willows, stagnant ditches, battery pits and
torn-up mounds; then, through zigzag cuttings in the marshy
ground containing tangles of signal wire, they reached the
trenches.

German troops behind the Flanders breastworks

The "trenches" in this low-lying, waterlogged, area were breastworks, ridges cast up on both sides of a shallow trench dug down to the water level. These earthen walls, capped with sandbags, were held in place by brushwood hurdles, corrugated iron and wired stakes and frames. Beneath the trench floor of boards and slats (duckboards) foul-smelling water sloshed about. Duties began with the "stand to arms" at first light, the likely hour for attack; then the protective wire was checked, to be thickened if need be the following night; the inspection of stores, rifles and localities followed; then housekeeping tasks such as the strengthening of breastworks were put in hand. At night patrols went out and, worst of all, listening-posts, pushed forward into the "devil's strip," were manned.

Allied breastworks in Flanders

Canadians return from Kitcheners Wood after heavy losses

Mobile post office and field kitchen behind the lines in Flanders

22

It was a quiet sector, but still the fresh troops felt the brooding presence of the front. New digging disclosed rusty metal, bones, rotting cloth and putrescent flesh. A good deal of lime was needed. The zone between the opposing trenches, often only forty yards apart, was bullet-beaten. Bullets zipped overhead or wailed in ricocheting agony from strands of wire and jagged metal. As yet the full possibilities of artillery had not been realized; a few shells would occasionally go screaming by. Others fell close at hand, prompting a quick "Get Down!" from experienced Tommies who had learned to interpret the deadly sounds; the ground was gouged into a shower of spouting mud; the parapet jumped and danced in bright explosions, while blasts of heated air and fragmented metal soughed and whined above. Bursts of Lewis gunfire or rifle grenades, which the Canadians were encouraged to fire, brought the instant response of bullets that smacked and flayed the sandbags.

Nights were a strange experience. German flares soared up to curve back to the ground or, suspended by parachute, sank slowly, distorting the torn landscape with eerie light and shadows. The enemy's parapet sprang out frighteningly close. Men caught in no-man's-land froze prone upon the ground until the light had died. But it was the want of sleep that struck the men most. Huddled on the raw wet firestep, they snatched what rest they could, legs brushed aside by passers-by, a rifle going off at the nearest slit, artillery rumbling in the distance, or friendly guns crashing out behind. Only a groundsheet protected them from the February snow and chilling rain, and then, stiff and weary, the morning "stand to arms" aroused them.

There were casualties that week, but no more than the normal "wastage" in the trenches. The dead were properly buried behind the lines by their shocked friends; death was not yet commonplace.

The elaborate war plans of Germany, France and Russia had been tried in 1914 and every one had failed. The success of heavy howitzers used by the Germans against the Belgian forts had been one of the early surprises of the war but, with gaps opening between their armies, Schlieffen's intention of encircling Paris had been departed from. The British Expeditionary Force was in position by 20 August, on the French left, centred on the Belgian town of Mons. There the Germans, on their massive, wheeling march, blundered into it on 23 August. Two British divisions stood off a force three times their strength by rapid rifle fire. Sir John French, the British commander, intended to stand firm and fight again next day.

The Second Battle of Ypres, from a painting by W. B. Wollen

A German machine-gun, the weapon which stultified Allied attacks throughout 1915 and 1916, positioned in the trenches

By June 1915 gas masks were common

25

General Alderson, decorating a Canadian after Second Ypres

But he was abandoned by the French, without notice, and so was forced to pull back that night. So began the long retreat from Mons which so disillusioned Sir John that he seriously contemplated leaving the French to their own devices.
The French and British, however, footsore and bone-weary from retreat, counter-attacked on the Marne, forcing the Germans to abandon their victorious sweep and fall back to the River Aisne. The French, in their bright red trousers and dark blue coats, had followed "Plan XVII" which called for an impetuous offensive into the provinces of Alsace and Lorraine (which they had lost to the Germans in 1871 as a result of the Franco-Prussian War) but this had been bloodily repulsed; in any case the attack had merely conformed to German strategy. The shabbily-equipped Russians planned to concentrate first against Austria, then deal with Germany when the ponderous Russian mobilization had been completed. But the French, heavily pressed, called for an immediate offensive against Germany. The Russians, who complied, tried to carry out two offensives, for which they were not ready, and they were disastrously defeated by relatively weak German forces in East Prussia.

Thereafter the opposing forces on the Western Front had tried to turn the other's flank. It had not proved possible and both sides reached the Swiss border and the sea. The British held the Germans from the Channel ports at the First Battle of Ypres.

French-Canadians in Flanders

27

The attack against the orchard at Festubert

In that fierce action the British regular army was virtually destroyed, a measure of what modern war could mean. From that time on new armies of volunteers, and later, conscripts, would carry on the struggle—the non-professional mass armies that were to come.

The Allies, in 1915, planned to break the deadlock on the Western Front. The time was surely opportune for that year the Germans stood on the defensive in the West while they concentrated against Russia in the East. Russia had been largely isolated from her western Allies by the entry of Turkey into the war on the German side. Thus the French, with British help, took the offensive against strong defences that were covered by artillery and machine-gun fire; the German lead in weaponry

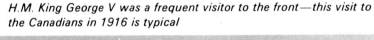

H.M. King George V was a frequent visitor to the front—this visit to the Canadians in 1916 is typical

Canadian Orchard, Festubert

had not yet been overtaken. Without the key to unlock the barrier, they achieved nothing and suffered badly. Some in Britain advocated a different policy. The true strategy for a maritime power, they argued, was to turn a flank by sea; to bring arms and ammunition to the poorly-equipped but numerically superior Russians, and not to fling men away against machine-guns and barbed wire. The plan was tried against Turkey at the Dardanelles, but it failed through poor planning and half-measures. It did, however, cause Italy, and partly influenced Roumania, to enter the war on the Allied side; Bulgaria sided with the Germans. The Newfoundland Regiment fought with the British at the Dardanelles but returned to the Western Front when the expedition was abandoned. From that time on, the major theatre was always France and Flanders.

Despite the Germans' strict defensive on the Western Front, local attacks were mounted. One of these, to screen the dispatch of the Eleventh German Army to the Russian front, was directed against the Ypres Salient. As this was the last Belgian ground in Allied hands, its retention was important. The 1st Division had marched into the Salient early in April, 1915; it was here that the Canadians received their baptism of fire in battle.

On 22 April, a lovely spring evening, the Germans struck at the Algerians, on the Canadian left. Contrary to the Hague Convention governing the conduct of warfare, they released the contents of 5,730 cylinders of chlorine gas which, borne on a light breeze, rolled in a writhing wall of olive-green vapour over the Algerian parapets. Without protection, men, their lungs seared, choked and died or—nauseated and powerfully sick—broke and fled leaving a gap in the Allied defences. The enemy, however, had had little faith in his powerful new weapon which unlocked four miles of front; he had not provided adequate reserves to exploit his great success. Thus, after a two-mile advance, the Germans hesitated, then paused to await the morning. Had they not done so but moved on Ypres—blazing from bombardment—they could have struck across the chord of the Salient to encircle 50,000 Canadian and British troops. It could, in fact, have been a tremendous victory.

Spring behind the lines in Flanders

That night Canadian troops worked desperately to close the gap. Lance-Corporal Frederick Fisher of the 13th Battalion, holding the Germans away from Canadian guns, won Canada's first Victoria Cross of the war.* Troops of the 3rd Brigade (commanded by Brig.-Gen. Richard Turner) who had never before been used in the attack, hurled themselves into the unknown at midnight and drove the enemy briefly out of Kitcheners Wood, an oak plantation near the village of St. Julien. Before daybreak, the Brigade was forced back—unable to recover its dead and wounded—with heavy losses. Turner then attacked twice by daylight and, though little ground was gained, his attacks upset the enemy; the Germans, bewildered by attacks when at the most they had expected a patchy defence, did not advance on the 23rd, as they had planned. That night the gap the gas had opened had been sealed.

The 24th marked the 1st Division's real ordeal. The day opened with a violent bombardment and another cloud of death, this time directed at the Canadians. The heaviest concentrations drifted over Brig.-Gen. Arthur Currie's 2nd Brigade whose men, using cotton bandoliers soaked in water for protection, coughed and choked in the acrid fumes with streaming eyes. Those who did not suffocate grimly held their ground despite their losses. Every German rush was held short of the parapets by accurate artillery and small-arms fire though the Ross, which jammed repeatedly during rapid fire, infuriated the harassed men; they tore at rifle bolts with bleeding hands, sobbing with exasperation.** The 3rd Brigade, on Currie's left, was literally blown out of its positions by German gunfire at short range; it relinquished St. Julien, and the shattered bodies of many

*The first V.C. to be won on the Western Front in 1915 was that of a Canadian, L/Cpl. Michael O'Leary, who was serving with the British Army.

** C.S.M. Frederick William Hall of the 8th Battalion won the V.C. for his attempts to retrieve a wounded comrade in this stern fighting.

31

Ruined Ypres

By 1915 the defensive wire had thickened

32

men, to the enemy. Lieutenant Edward Bellew, whose gallantry imposed delay on the advancing Germans, won another V.C. A fourth went to a medical officer, Captain Alexander Caron Scrimger, for his devotion to the wounded throughout the battle. The line was stabilized 600 yards south of St. Julien and the divisional front, though viciously and repeatedly attacked, stood firm throughout the day. Towards evening British reinforcements brought relief to the grimy, battle-worn troops and the Salient, though smaller now, remained in Allied hands.

Canada, in this first defensive battle, had written her name large above the fens of Ypres; her men had been tested now and they had proved a match for German professionals. That week the fame of Canadian soldiers redounded around the world. "These splendid troops," wrote Sir John French, "averted a disaster" and so they had. The price was heavy—more than six thousand Canadians killed and wounded. Well might the carnage wrought near Ypres stir Major John McCrae to write: "In Flanders fields the poppies blow, Between the crosses, row on row..."

Ypres has since been restored

Though the Second Battle of Ypres continued for three more weeks only one Canadian battalion was engaged. The Princess Patricia's, as part of the British 27th Division, helped stem a German advance from Frezenberg Ridge on 8 May. That day they suffered almost four hundred casualties in an heroic stand. The fighting died down and thereafter, for the next two years, the line around the Salient remained virtually unchanged.

It was the Allies, not the Germans, who carried out the major offensives of 1915. In May the British attacked in Artois, to divert attention from the French (now wearing more sober uniforms of horizon blue), who unsuccessfully stormed Vimy Ridge. The 1st Division, whose losses after Ypres had been made good by men from the Cavalry Brigade who had volunteered to fight as infantry, fought at Festubert in May and at Givenchy in June. The objectives were all taken but these were minor; there never was a grand sweep forward by the Allies. One more V.C. was won, by Lieutenant Frederick William Campbell of the 1st Battalion, at Givenchy. This small battle was nevertheless significant for Canadian infantrymen of the 1st Division. In it they carried the short Lee-Enfield rifle. The Ross was no longer used by any Canadian troops, apart from a few for snipers, after August, 1916.

Gunfire, used to cut the enemy wire, had forewarned the opposing troops in these battles of 1915. As yet there were no rolling barrages to screen the attackers who stumbled over the torn-up ground while machine-guns cut them down. The fighting in Artois cost Canada 2,468 casualties at Festubert and, at Givenchy, four hundred more. Yet the pathetic bodies in no-man's-land were to little purpose; men died striving for a breakthrough that was unattainable with the equipment and the tactics available. The over-optimistic Allied generals, who saw only the unspoiled fields beyond and not the impregnability of the defensive lines—and who still hurled men forward in one useless attack after another—must be held to blame.

The French commander, Joffre—a short, fat man with a large mustache—was not discouraged by the results of the offensives he had planned. He was satisfied that "nibbling" would achieve results in time and closed his eyes to the enormous casualties;

The Ross, 1914

No. 2 Stationary Hospital was the first Canadian hospital in France

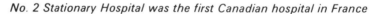

50,000 French in Champagne during February; 60,000 at
St. Mihiel; in May 100,000 more at Arras and on Vimy Ridge.
He believed that the French, the British and the Russians, with
their reserves of manpower, were like gamblers holding a huge
bankroll. Sooner or later their resources would prevail. They must
attack and attack. Losses were immaterial provided the Germans
were made to pay even a percentage of the Allied losses.
German manpower would some day be exhausted. Thus was
born the horrible policy of attrition. Like Joffre, Sir John French
too remained undaunted. He had ordered "deliberate and
persistent" attacks by which the enemy would be "gradually
and relentlessly worn down by exhaustion and loss until his
defence collapses." One of these attacks had been Festubert
about which Currie, a thoughtful man, had been deeply
concerned. After the battle he had written, "I received the
message 'Well done, 2nd Brigade,' but while such messages are
deeply appreciated, they do not console. There I lost 53 officers
and 1,200 men."

The Short Lee Enfield, 1914

Arthur Currie

35

Why not stay on the defensive, it may well be asked, and await technological advances such as the tank which appeared in 1916? In the emotional atmosphere of those times the politicians and the public would hardly have tolerated a defensive strategy. In 1915 only the Germans could afford to fight defensively. They held large areas of Allied territory. The Allies, on the other hand, were committed to drive the Germans out. The Allied generals had armies to use and so they used them offensively, as they were expected to do. And so wave after wave of men were sent "over the top" and into no-man's-land in the face of machine-guns and artillery to tackle the German wire and trenches. Sometimes they captured whole sections of the opposing front line; some even got as far as the second line of trenches. But it was seldom possible to retain even a foothold in the face of counter-attack. If the attack were bold enough and committed enough men, some would get through. In the long run the gains were nil or small and tremendously costly. Thus we have the spectacle of over-confident generals in chateaux far behind the lines, pointing to the map and ordering a thrust here or there to straighten out an untidy line; and then that of the men, like warrior ants, moving blindly forward towards sure disaster. Thousands died and achieved nothing by it. Therein lies the horror and the fascination of the First World War.

At the end of the year the stalemate that had settled on the Western Front remained unbroken. Sir John French was dismissed to be succeeded by Sir Douglas Haig, a man of soldierly appearance and with a keen sense of duty. Haig had no more idea how to cope with the deadlock than anybody else but he was supremely confident that, with Divine help, he would somehow find a way.

Nor had Germany achieved her ends in 1915; Russia had been driven back three hundred miles but, though badly mauled, she fought on. The Germans still had to cope with a two-front war.

36

Part Three:
A Corps for Canada:
The First Fighting for the
2nd, 3rd, and 4th Divisions

Courtesy of the National Gallery of Canada   *—Painted by Kenneth Forbes*

THE DEFENCE OF SANCTUARY WOOD

In Canada the enthusiasm which had greeted the outbreak of the
war led to the offer of a second contingent three days after
the first had sailed. Twenty thousand strong, it crossed the
Atlantic in the spring of 1915; the 2nd Division was formed from
it in May and in September the new division moved to France.
At the wish of Canada an army corps—the Canadian Corps—
of the 1st and 2nd Divisions was then formed under Alderson's
command. Currie took Alderson's place in the 1st Division;
Turner commanded the 2nd.

These men were very different. Turner was lean, scholarly
looking, with spectacles. Despite his appearance, which was
not that of a typical soldier, he had won the Victoria Cross—

37

the highest award for bravery—in South Africa. Currie was a big solid man, whose cap sat squarely above a long, heavily jowled face. A non-professional soldier, thoughtful and phlegmatic, he was destined to command the Canadian Corps as the "ablest Corps Commander in the British Forces."

By this time it was clear to British and Dominion eyes that the relatively small land forces they had furnished in 1914 were but the advance guard of the nation. Continental warfare, on the scale of this struggle, demanded more than the regulars, reserves and small Dominion contingents that had previously been used in war; nothing less than the total commitment of the "nation in arms" could hope to prevail over the national armies of the Central Powers that were based on universal service and backed by industrial mobilization. In January, 1916, Britain ordered compulsory military service for single men. Firmly resolved, Canada faced reality and prepared to play her part but without conscription as yet.

A Flanders farm

One of the craters at Saint-Eloi, photographed three years after the explosion

Sandbag and corrugated iron revetments in the Canadian trenches

The ward of a Field Ambulance in 1916

THE SOMME

Courcelette

Repair shop

Heavy artillery

Ammunition train

Between December, 1915 and October, 1916 the small British Expeditionary Force had become 49 infantry divisions and five cavalry divisions, organized in five armies, and Canadian growth, proportionately, matched this expansion; Canada sent a third and fourth division to the Western Front and formed a fifth in England. The 3rd Division came into being in December, 1915, under Maj.-Gen. M. S. Mercer, formerly of the 1st Brigade. To it came the Princess Patricia's, after a year's service with the British, and the Royal Canadian Regiment which had served in Bermuda. The 4th, commanded by Maj.-Gen. David Watson, crossed to France from England in August 1916. The 5th Division was later formed in England but it never served as such in France. All four divisions on the Western Front were grouped together in the Canadian Corps which, with this steady augmentation, was to become a sturdy representative of its country and, in fact, a national force.

The new Corps, consisting at first of the 1st and 2nd Divisions, spent the autumn and winter on the familiar Flanders front. Infantry reinforcements had made it possible to return the cavalrymen (who had served as infantry) to the Cavalry Brigade. Though the great offensives of 1915 in Artois and Champagne had petered out, an aggressive spirit was fostered for the Canadians by trench-raids on an increasing scale. These died away with winter.

Raindrops dripped from rusting wire; the churned-up earth in no-man's-land turned to mud; shell holes and craters brimmed with water. And the trenches, gouged into the low-lying ground, filled like the ditches they were. The troops, hunched under glistening groundsheets in the slanting rain, stood thigh-deep in water behind the dissolving breastworks. The enemy, on higher ground, was better off; and, to discommode his opponents still further, he drained his trenches—including sewage—in the Canadian direction.

Signals

Advanced post

41

Sentry

Fixing bayonets

Over the top

Lieutenant-General the Hon. Sir Julian Byng

High rubber boots were issued, but there were not enough to go round; "trench feet," arising from the cold and wet and an added infection from the soil, set in. As with frostbite, feet swelled and tissues deteriorated and would become gangrenous if not checked. Colds, influenza and even pneumonia were common; rats and lice were ever present. There was no warmth, no comfort, even in the shattered leaky billets behind the lines. Only the daily rum ration, Christmas Day and the arrival of the 3rd Division were briefly cheering.

Spring came, and with it the first fighting for the 2nd Division. General Sir Herbert Plumer, commanding the Second British Army, decided to straighten out a small salient at St. Eloi which thrust into the British line. For this he named the British 3rd Division which attacked on 27 March, 1916, after blowing six mines under the enemy's position. The ground rose, broke with a roar, and then earth was shot into the air, blotting out the sun. The British occupied the area while the clods still rained down. On 4 April the 2nd Division, the first Canadians to wear the newly-introduced steel helmets in battle, took over the defence of the mine craters from the British and manned the sodden forward line. The men dug and wired and squatted down to eat "bully" and "hardtack" in the mud. On the morning of 6 April, before the British gains had been fully consolidated, the Germans counter-attacked and regained every crater save one. It was now the turn of the Canadians to attack and a stubborn see-saw battle developed (with the Canadians holding two of the craters which had been lost) which lasted for 13 days. Then, on 19 April, shells screeched down on the waterlogged ground during a three-hour bombardment and the Germans finally drove the dazed defenders out. Only one crater remained in Canadian hands and the price paid for that hole had been 1,373 killed, wounded and missing men. After the Canadian failure at St. Eloi, Alderson, whose open criticism of the Ross rifle had upset Hughes in Canada, was replaced as Corps Commander by another British officer, Lieut.-Gen. the Hon. Sir Julian Byng.

A visit by Hughes—Seely, the Canadian Cavalry Brigade commander, is second from the left, and Sir Max Aitken (later Lord Beaverbrook) is on the right

The Somme battlefield

German wounded

Wounded Canadians

The tank made its appearance at the Somme

Byng's appointment was popular with the troops. "This," reported one officer, "is a soldier—large, strong, lithe, with worn boots and frayed puttees. He carries his hand in his pocket, and returns a salute by lifting his hand as far as the pocket will allow." His informality was to the Canadian taste, and the men responded. It is not surprising that Byng became a Governor-General of Canada in the post-war years.

The Canadian Corps spent the summer in the Ypres Salient, but it was no holiday idyll. The area, as always, was evil. A maze of trenches dissected the ground, many dating back to the old 1914 and 1915 fighting and in a state of disrepair, while all of them were laden with "a distillation of appalling stenches". In the area north of Ypres-Comines Canal, one Canadian battalion took over a trench still "choked with the decomposed bodies of Scottish soldiers".

Enemy shelling was violent. *Minenwerfer* (trench mortars) lobbed projectiles like small rum barrels onto the frail breastworks with devastating effect. Bullets whipped and cracked from all directions, some even entering the parapets from the wrong side, for this was the Ypres Salient and could be ranged on by German guns and small-arms from around the semi-circle. And there was the ever-present danger of whole sections of trench leaping skywards through enemy mine-workings underneath. Even digging in dud-infested ground took its toll. There was no safety anywhere.

There was no longer any optimism about an early victory. The first year had done no more than stem the German tide; 1915 had seen strong defensive lines develop that could be held by relatively weak enemy forces, and still could not be broken through; and 1916 might well see the speedy transfer of enemy troops that, having dulled the Russian steel, could be hurled once more against the West. The earlier enthusiasm had by now abated. Despite journalistic eulogies boosting near-disasters into far-reaching victories, returning wounded had reported otherwise. The men of the 3rd Division, though still untried, had talked to the veterans of the 1st—and those of the 2nd so recently "blooded" at St. Eloi. They had no illusions.

An impression of the bitter struggle for the Sugar Refinery, Courcelette

Wounded

Prisoners

The dead

Sympathy for fellow sufferers   *Endurance*

Byng conducted his first Corps' battle at Mount Sorrel in June, 1916. In it, the 3rd Division experienced its first action. On the morning of June 2nd a day-old enemy bombardment increased in fury to become the heaviest yet experienced by Canadian troops. A four-hour eruption of black shrapnel bursts and sulphurous spouts of earth told of the agony of the 3rd Division. Human bodies, even the trees of Sanctuary Wood, were hurled skywards by the bursting shells. It is names like Sanctuary Wood that recall the grim humour of the front-line soldiers, for there was little sanctuary there that day. Those who were not blown apart were smothered in earth and dust; or they were spattered with blood, bone and flesh from the hideous body fragments that hurtled through the air. German infantry—advancing confidently, almost leisurely, in their grey-green uniforms— then attacked. The 3rd Division, in the line, was overrun and its commander (Mercer) killed by shrapnel. Three hills—Mount Sorrel, Hill 61 and 62—were all lost and hills were important in Flanders. Two Canadian guns, for the first and only time in the war, were also lost but they were recovered before the battle ended.

48

By nightfall the German advance was checked. A counter-attack by the 1st Division at dawn met with no success. Then, on the 6th, the Germans rounded out their gains by capturing the village of Hooge after exploding four mines; but as this entailed the loss of only a few yards, Byng ignored it. The hills were a different matter. He determined to win them back and once again he named Currie's 1st Division. This time he gave Currie time for careful planning and by the 12th everything was ready. The attack would be launched at night, following a heavy artillery bombardment.

The assault—sharp and brilliantly successful—began soon after midnight on 13 June. The well-rehearsed troops of the 1st Division went straight to their objectives despite the darkness and the wind and rain. The heights lost on 2 June were all re-taken and the Canadians consolidated on the old front line which Allied artillery had badly shattered; what had once been a system of trenches had been obliterated. Though the battle cost some eight thousand casualties, it was a clear-cut victory for the Corps.

The German advantage of interior lines had been demonstrated in 1914 and in 1915; the enemy had switched troops from the Eastern and the Western Fronts at will. This, the Allies planned, would be nullified in 1916 by mounting simultaneous offensives on the Western, Eastern and Italian fronts so that the enemy could not disengage to any large extent. In the West the French and British were to carry out a joint offensive at the Somme scheduled for the beginning of August.

Joffre had pointed to the Somme, where the British and French lines joined. The area offered no strategical prize. In fact, the territory favoured the Germans who were firmly entrenched in the chalky uplands. The Allies would be attacking uphill. The site, however, was convenient in that the French and British were already adjacent there; and an offensive would bring on heavy fighting that would kill a lot of Germans. Haig, who had criticized Sir John French's offensive methods, favoured this combined offensive. Kitchener's "New Army" was steadily arriving and by August he would have a mighty force of almost sixty divisions. Once again it was not strategy but a policy of attrition.

Evacuation

The relief of firm ground

Ruined Albert

50

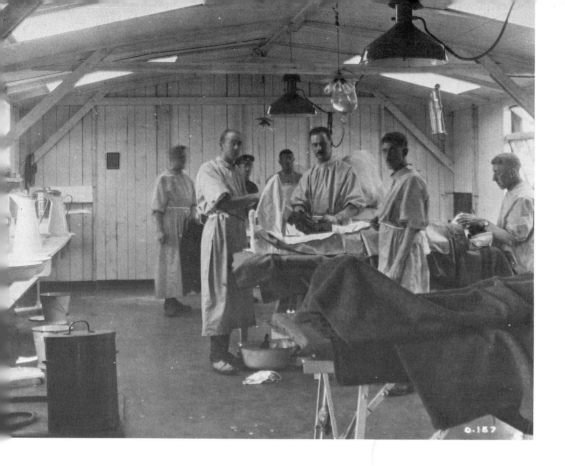

Recuperation

The Germans dislocated the Anglo-French scheme by striking first. Falkenhayn, who had replaced von Moltke after the failure of the Schlieffen Plan, chose to attack Verdun. He chose this place because it was a fortress-symbol that would be defended by the French. Once tied to Verdun by pride, the French armies would be bled to death by gunfire. Thus the Germans too adopted a policy of attrition. With such generalship on both sides, it promised to be an even more futile and bloody war than it had been before.

The Verdun battle opened on 21 February, 1916, and the German offensive continued for seven months. A French counter-offensive followed, which extended the fighting until 15 December, a duration record even by the "impossible" standards of the First World War. In the old days decisive battles were fought in hours. This one, in which early German gains were finally wiped out by the French, was indecisive; it merely demonstrated that a state of balance existed between the Central Powers and the Allies in terms of industrial resources.

Falkenhayn's concept was proved correct. Verdun was indeed a symbol that the French would not relinquish. But to the Germans the fortress became a symbol, too, which *had* to be captured; thus both became imprisoned in its horror.

The French front collapsed under the impact of more than three thousand guns. Falkenhayn had seen enough of the failure of Allied mass attacks not to imitate their methods. Only small probing parties would go forward after the annihilating barrage to report on the next line of resistance; this would then become the target for renewed artillery bombardment. Pétain was rushed to the scene and took command on 25 February. Reinforcements and two thousand French guns poured in. The battle dragged on for week after week of vast artillery duels. But inevitably the infantry on both sides were drawn into the mutually destroying process of attack and counter-attack. By June, two-thirds of the French Army (sixty-six divisions out of a hundred) had passed through the "furnace" of Verdun, and yet by the end of the month the Germans had amalgamated enough miniscule amounts of ground to be almost in possession of the fortress.

The battle continues

Outside events then made their influence felt. On 4 June Russia, crippled but not defeated, loyally attacked to take the pressure off France as she had done briefly and unsuccessfully in March. This time the offensive continued throughout June and was resumed in August. It carried the Russians to the Carpathians, the last barrier to the Hungarian plain. There the Germans stemmed it. Russian success, however, compelled Falkenhayn to detach troops from the Western Front; it forced the Austrians to abandon an offensive against the Italians; it encouraged Roumania to enter the war on the Allied side and that led to the dismissal of Falkenhayn. But all this had been wrought at a heavy price. Russia never again played a significant part in the war; the sequel was revolution and collapse in 1917.

By midsummer France was in no position to shoulder any major burden at the Somme. In advising Haig, Joffre appealed for the date of the offensive to be advanced to 1 July. Haig accepted this and on 24 June the preparatory bombardment for the relief offensive on the Somme began. A day later Falkenhayn stopped the flow of divisions and munitions to Verdun; and in the autumn the French wrested from the Germans the ground that they had won. At Verdun, in the final account, Germany lost almost as heavily as France.

53

The trophy

54

At the Somme, Haig counted on massive artillery concentrations to crush the enemy's defences, but, at the moment of attack, the artillery lifted off to targets farther back. Moving barrages were still unknown. The German front-line defenders, immune in deep dugouts, then emerged to cut down the infantry with machine-gun fire while artillery shells assisted in the work of slaughter. Bullets and shrapnel struck home and limbs were torn away. Arms reached out in agony; men collapsed in death; or badly wounded, rolled and twitched on the spouting ground. Others, less severely injured dragged themselves into shell holes seeking shelter. The uninjured, grimy but remorseless as dripping water, closed ranks and stumbled on to close with the enemy. Thus the morning of 1 July, 1916, witnessed a disaster unequalled in the annals of British arms— 57,500 men killed, wounded or missing in a few short hours under the cloudless skies of Picardy. The soldiers' song, "Roses are blooming in Picardy," became a mockery that day. The Newfoundland Regiment alone, thrusting forward near Beaumont Hamel, suffered 710 casualties and at home 1 July is still a day of mourning.

Haig, a stubborn Scot, nevertheless persisted,* and by the end of November the British had butted forward six miles on a ten-mile front. Though the cost was enormous it is generally accepted now that German losses were about the same. There is no doubt that the Somme relieved Verdun; it forced the Germans to relax their pressure and made the French counter-strokes possible. Some of the advances at the Somme were due to tanks though the wisdom of using them before numbers were ready may be doubted; this great strategic surprise—as with the use of gas by the Germans at Second Ypres—was thrown away for trifling gains. Fortunately, although Haig ordered a thousand tanks, the Germans were not impressed by their performance and devoted scant attention to this form of mechanized warfare.

The Canadians, inevitably, were drawn into the holocaust, where three more V.Cs. were won: by Corporal Leo Clarke, of the 2nd Battalion; by Private John Chipman Kerr of the 49th; and by Piper James Cleland Richardson of the 16th Battalion. In the middle of July the Canadian Cavalry Brigade took part in the attack on Bazentin Ridge. In September the Canadian Corps joined the fighting. The 1st Division drove the enemy from his remaining positions on Pozières Ridge and here, while relieving the Australian and New Zealand Army Corps, one Canadian brigade (the 3rd) suffered 970 casualties. This was an indication

*In the renewed fighting, a Canadian, Lt. T. O. L. Wilkinson, won the V.C. on 5 July while serving with the British Army.

Prisoners assist

Making a cross

of what future fighting at the Somme would mean. The Pozières feature was cleared on 11 September and Haig decided to deliver a renewed blow with all his resources at the middle of the month. By then the newly-invented British tank was ready for trial in action and seven were allocated to the Canadian front.

The British attack was delivered by two armies on 15 September. The Canadian Corps advanced against the village of Courcelette, part of what was to become known as the Battle of Flers-Courcelette, with the 2nd Division in the major role. The tanks proved helpful to the attacking infantry. Despite mechanical failures and the torn up ground, one tank reached the objective, an outer bastion of the Courcelette and Martinpuich defences known as the Sugar Factory; this was taken by the infantry after a brief hand-to-hand struggle in an inferno of grenade and machine-gun fire. The Canadians then

56

made a bid for Courcelette. A sunken road crowded with machine-guns barred the way but the attackers moved through a welter of dead and dying men to sweep it clear with the bayonet; by evening they had seized Courcelette. The 26th Battalion mopped up the town and suffered badly. That night the Germans counter-attacked again and again—seven attacks against the 22nd Battalion of French Canadians and four against the 25th Battalion of Nova Scotians—and there were more next day. The gains were held.

On the left the 3rd Division (under Maj.-Gen. Lipsett, who had succeeded Mercer), strongly supported by the 1st Motor Machine Gun Brigade, had secured a portion of the strongly-defended Fabeck Trench in the first day's fighting. It cleared the remainder next day.

The fighting which had begun on 15 September gained two miles. Thereafter momentum waned and a stiff price was paid for every yard of ground. On the 22nd, with enemy resistance mounting, Haig called off the battle. He considered it essential, however, to clear the whole of the crest-line of the high ground overlooking the river Ancre and fighting resumed on Thiepval Ridge towards the end of September. This was followed by the Battle of the Ancre Heights which began in October. The target for the Corps during this period was the next German defence line beyond Courcelette—Regina Trench.

On 1 October the 3rd Division made an attempt to take Regina Trench. As yet no artillery fuse had been designed to cut barbed wire and the attack stalled in the enemy's entanglements. Only a handful of men reached the trench, to lay grey-green German forms asprawl, but they were beaten back. Another attack, carried out by the 1st and 3rd Divisions on 8 October, though heavily pressed, also failed. It was the same story of machine-guns and uncut wire. By this time the Canadian Corps was exhausted.

Shattered objectives

It was the same with the other troops—British or Dominion—
who fought at the Somme. They had had their Calvaries.
Newfoundland at Beaumont-Hamel; South Africa among the
shattered stumps of Delville Wood; Australia and New Zealand
at Pozières and Villers-Bretonneux; and Britain on too many
ghastly fields to name. The grandeur and power of Lutyens'
massive arches, high on Thiepval Ridge, today sum up the
emotion of what was then the British Empire. The memorial
bears the names of 74,000 missing dead.

Too much blood had flowed and the might, the wealth and
the pomp of the Empire was fading. But wounded Canadian
soldiers, convalescing from the Somme, could hardly notice that
in London. There was the customary business and the traffic
flowed unaltered. Young ladies, in white dresses, sauntered
in the parks. The city followed its accustomed course and yet
the course, imperceptibly, was changing. Britain's treasure,
in men and money, was being rapidly consumed and the
old certainty gone forever. The heavily-censored war news was
invariably good. The fighting on the Somme and at Verdun
showed "an uninterrupted series of successes." Facts were
concealed. It was felt in every country that if the people knew
the truth about the war they would no longer support it.
Yet the "Roll of Honour" carried in all the newspapers was
always full of the names of dead, wounded and missing men—
as many as 4,000 for the last twenty-four hours, overflowing
onto other pages. After a meal of egg and chips there was
pleasure to pursue: Music Hall; *Peg O' My Heart* at the Globe;
The Rotters at the Strand; and beer and spirits in the rowdy pubs.
Men from the front made the most of leave in "Blighty."

Observation balloon at the Somme

The 4th Division, which had not yet been in battle, reached the Somme on 10 October. On 17 October the Canadian Corps, with the exception of the 4th Division and the artillery of the other three divisions, left the Somme for a quiet sector of the front facing Vimy Ridge. It was left to the 4th Division to take Regina Trench and its supports, Desire Trench, after the rest of the Corps had left the battle area.

In carrying out these tasks the 4th Division experienced the dreadful conditions that are always associated with the Somme. It was a nightmare of the foulest sort. The inexperienced troops were suddenly pitchforked into the obscenities of modern war in a battle of attrition against the strongest defences. They were pitted against German troops whose orders were explicit: any officer who gave up an inch of trench would be court-martialed; and any sector of lost trench must be counter-attacked immediately. This order of Falkenhayn's, typical of Haig's in obstinacy, made for stern fighting; but it also subjected the Germans to severe losses. Added to that, from October on, the weather had broken, turning the battleground into a morass, littered with the fragments of men who had been blown to pieces.

Sad river mists filled the valleys, spangling khaki with cold raw dew. On the exposed ridges drizzling rain turned the grey-white chalk to treacherous slime. The low sun hardly shone through the gloomy skies. The rain persisted and the mud deepened to a mortar-like consistency that filled the trenches and oozed down dugout entrances. Shell holes and craters became small lakes of grey "cement" or were turned brown by rust and blood. Bodies in strange attitudes and useless gear lay in pathetic bundles on the stripped and wasted ground.

Over that ground the men attacked "loaded with more cold iron than a gaol would give a murderer". Shells snouted up the greyish mud in showers or skidded sickeningly on the limb-strewn ground. Soldiers sobbed with frustration as they tore themselves out of the muck, which packed and balled on the foot like slushy snow, and floundered forward. When they fell, as they often did, clothing and equipment got plastered with mud and grew heavier. Some blundered head deep into shell holes and were left screaming to their fate. And never before, except at Verdun, had so many shells saturated any battlefield.

Only the best of men in such conditions could go in and win. The 4th Division did that at the Somme.

Crosses on the shell-torn battlefield

General Robert Nivelle

At the end of November, when the 4th rejoined the Corps which had moved to the Vimy front, there had been more than 24,000 Canadian casualties in the Battles of the Somme and the end was not in sight. In January, 1916, Canada had sent 120,000 soldiers overseas; a year later, another 165,000 had gone and total enlistments in Canada, at that time, had grown to 400,000. Casualty lists lengthened in newspapers across the land. Every community was affected in some way by the war and yet the resolve of the country remained unshaken.

Joffre, whose "strategy" had brought 1,300,000 casualties to France by December, 1916, and who had foreseen no danger at Verdun, had lost the confidence of the nation. In mid-December he was promoted Marshal and "retired" as Commander-in-Chief. His successor was Robert Nivelle, who had replaced Pétain at Verdun and conducted the successful French counter-offensive in the fall, and who now promised certain victory.

Haig alone remained, secure in his position as Commander-in-Chief of the British armies. Early in 1917 the King promoted him to Field Marshal "as a New Year's gift from myself and the country."

Beaumont Hamel was finally captured—this had been the railway station

Part Four:
Winning the Heights:
Vimy—Hill 70—Passchendaele

Courtesy of the National Gallery of Canada *—Painted by Richard Jack*

THE TAKING OF VIMY RIDGE, EASTER MONDAY, 1917

At the end of 1916 the deadlock still persisted. The contenders
on the Western Front had fought themselves to a standstill in
battles of attrition. The Italians had made some gains against the
Austrians across the Isonzo. In June the Russians, in their
greatest contribution of the war, drove five Austrian armies
back a distance of twenty to thirty miles on a 300-mile front;
they then made good progress towards the Carpathians and
repulsed a Turkish invasion of the Caucasus. But neither Italy nor
Russia had saved Roumania, which, like Serbia the year before,
had been overrun.

 Falkenhayn's lack of success at Verdun and at the Somme—
Roumania's entry into the war was given as the official reason—

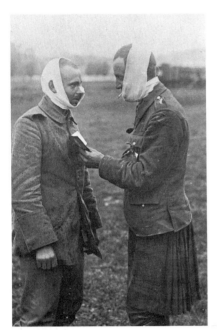

Trench raids, to obtain prisoners for the identification of units, were common

had led to his dismissal on 29 August, 1916. His successors, Hindenburg and his co-commander Ludendorff, shared Falkenhayn's opinion that a decision must be reached in the west, but they were not prepared to undergo another *Blutbad* at the Somme even though that had been a blood bath for the Allies, too. One of their first acts was to start the construction of a strong position further back, the Hindenburg Line, a shorter and straighter line that would be more defensible with fewer troops. Rather than await a second battering in the spring of 1917, they relinquished ground and withdrew to the Hindenburg Line. Though the line bore Hindenburg's name, Ludendorff was the real brain of the combination; Hindenburg has been well described as a "wooden titan."

The Corps occupied a fairly quiet sector opposite Vimy Ridge. The winter was cold, the hardest for twenty-two years, and the little Souchez River froze two feet thick; food, served hot, congealed to ice at the edge of mess-tins before it could be eaten. Nevertheless, despite the miseries, conditions were better than the year before. The trenches, which drained into the Zouave Valley, were reasonably dry, and the men had time to dig shelters in the chalk or frozen clay. There were the usual lice—and rats, which, gorged on human remains, grew to enormous size.

Anti-aircraft precautions were maintained

Behind the lines, concert parties occasionally entertained the men in converted barns. Some of these parties were later grouped into the "Dumbells", organized from serving soldiers of the 3rd Division; they entertained in France and became well known throughout Canada after the war. The parties sang music-hall songs, danced, and gave skits based on army life; they even included female impersonators. A song that sent cheers and laughter echoing from the smoky beams was sung by a man wearing full equipment: tin hat, rifle, bayonet, grenades, entrenching tool, haversack, pack, water bottle, rubber boots slung over his shoulder, and gas mask. He shuffled on stage wearing an expression of mingled gloom, misery and disgust, pushed his tin hat foward onto his nose and sang in the most dismal possible way:

> I've got a mott-er,
> Always merry and bright.

The favourite songs of this period were no longer jingoistic or patriotic; they were "Oh, What a Lovely War" and "Pack up Your Troubles in Your Old Kit-Bag."

The Dumbells

Hauling heavy shells

A cook and helper

A support trench on the Vimy front

During the German withdrawal to the Hindenburg Line, only the children, the old and infirm were left

A welcome coffee break on the Vimy front

65

General Robert Nivelle proposed a grandiose offensive for 1917. Using the counter-offensive methods of Verdun, he would break through the German lines and win the war. He never revealed much about his secret formula for victory, but he was young, handsome and energetic. He spoke good English and so impressed the new British Prime Minister, Lloyd George, that Haig was subordinated to Nivelle for the offensive. But the Germans disrupted Nivelle's plan by withdrawing to the Hindenburg Line after thoroughly devastating the countryside. In a belt, sometimes fifty miles wide, everything had been systematically wrecked. Houses had been blown up, roads cratered, wells poisoned, and even fruit trees felled. This restricted Nivelle's attack to a point south of the wasted area and the Hindenburg system and there the Germans prepared to meet him; nevertheless the French commander-in-chief proceeded blindly with his plan.

The British Fourth and Fifth Armies found themselves out of touch with the Germans after the withdrawal and crossed the wasted area to close with the new defences. The Canadian Cavalry Brigade took part in the Fourth Army's advance. Lieutenant F. M. W. Harvey, Lord Strathcona's Horse, who captured a machine-gun, won the V.C. on 27 March.

The British were to fight north of the devasted area, in the Arras sector, to keep the Germans occupied and thereby aid Nivelle. Haig ordered an attack by the British Third Army on an eight-mile front astride the Scarpe; and just north of that, an attack by the Canadian Corps to capture Vimy Ridge. Byng, who had ample time for planning, made careful preparations. By far the most important of these concerned the guns.

Better artillery methods had been born of the frustration at the Somme. In the limited time available the secret for a successful offensive under First World War conditions called for a devasting artillery blow to crush a section of the enemy's defences and then for the infantry to pass through to roll up the flanks. Previously the gunfire had preceded the movement

Orchards were felled ...

and roads cratered when the Germans withdrew

66

Men who were holding Vimy Ridge—and one who helped to take it

Villages were thoroughly devastated before the Germans pulled back to the Hindenburg Line

Training to use the enemy's artillery

Consolidating the newly won Ridge

of the attacking troops, and this, as on 1 July at the Somme, had given the enemy warning of attack. For Vimy the artillery would shoot close over the heads of the troops as they stormed forward, putting down a barrage of shells in front of them to screen their advance; at the same time newly-introduced "counter-battery" fire from other guns would paralyze the enemy's batteries when the attacking troops were in the greatest danger. And at Vimy, for the first time, a new instantaneous fuse for cutting wire was used.

The attack was scheduled for Easter Monday, 9 April, 1917, and on 20 March the preparatory bombardment began. This strengthened on 2 April when thousands upon thousands of shells rushed overhead to herald what the Germans termed "the week of suffering." On the night of 8 April the troops, guided by luminous stakes, moved quietly forward to assembly areas where a hot meal and rum issue were waiting. An early moon, just past the full, clouded over as the night wore on; in darkness the men filed through gaps in the Canadian wire to occupy jumping-off positions in no-man's-land. Shortly before dawn on the 9th, in snow and sleet, the infantry of all four divisions of the powerful Canadian Corps sprang off together all along the front. Simultaneously, with exquisite timing, the intensive fixed bombardment

A respite after the Ridge was won

Canadian cavalry moving forward

The frost-hardened ground of the Ridge melted as the day wore on

Storming Vimy Ridge . . .

. . . and digging in

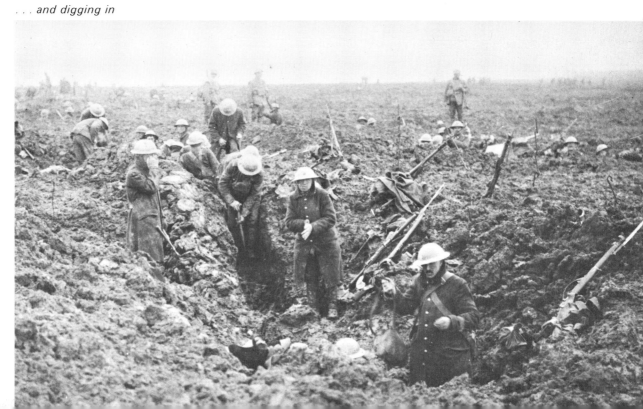

Tending German wounded on the battlefield

yielded first place to a rolling barrage, stiffened by machine-gun fire, that covered the men's advance. There was no slackening in the thunder of the guns to warn the enemy. The gentle forward slope of the ridge was soon a turmoil of moving men, spouting earth, drifting smoke and driving sleet. The infantry, to their satisfaction, found the majority of defenders in the forward defences still below ground and, what was more, the wire cut. German distress rockets brightened the morning gloom but the artillery response was weak as well it might be; during each phase of the attack Canadian counter-battery fire bombarded every enemy battery position known to be still active with gas shells and high explosive.

Once the forward defences had been overrun resistance stiffened. Well-concealed snipers and machine-guns, firing from concrete strongpoints, took their toll. Platoon tactics came into their own. Men dropped to engage them from the front with rapid fire while others, taking advantage of the broken ground, skirted round to seize them, using bayonets and grenades from flank and rear. Three V.Cs. were won — by Captain Thain Wendell MacDowell (38th Battalion), Private William Johnstone Milne (16th Battalion) and Lance-Sergeant Ellis Wellwood Sifton (18th Battalion) — in this tougher phase. Yet by 8 A.M. the 3rd Division had reached the foot of the ridge on the other side. The 2nd and the 1st Divisions, whose advance was longer, came into line in mid-afternoon. The outcome was no longer in doubt. Though the 4th Division on the left was held up by the highest feature of the ridge, which was strongly held, Vimy Ridge was completely won on 12 April. On the 10th, another V.C. was won, by Private John George Pattison, of the 50th Battalion. On the night of the 12th the Germans pulled back across the Douai Plain, leaving one of their strongest bastions on the Western Front in Canadian hands. The Battle of Vimy Ridge — a Canadian battle — was the greatest victory of the war up to that time.

Prisoners

Cleaning up

Prisoners file back

Four thousand prisoners, 54 guns, 104 trench mortars and 124 machine-guns were captured at a cost of 3,598 fatal casualties. Today Canada's most eloquent memorial to her dead stands high on Vimy Ridge.

The Third Army, fighting at the Scarpe on the Canadian right, had been equally successful but Nivelle's offensive, for which all this was a preliminary, failed. His battle opened on 16 April and, instead of the deep penetration he confidently expected, a gain of only four miles had been achieved when it was broken off on 9 May. By the end of the month the French armies, which had been keyed-up to expect success, seethed in open mutiny. Meanwhile, to assist Nivelle, Haig had kept up relentless pressure north and south of Arras against small villages of no strategic value. They became slaughter yards. Two of them, Arleux and Fresnoy, were seized by the Canadians in some of the hardest fighting of the war. Lieutenant Robert Grierson Combe, of the 27th Battalion, won the V.C. on 3 May. Nivelle had not performed his miracle. He was replaced by a prudent general, Pétain, who advocated a defensive strategy.

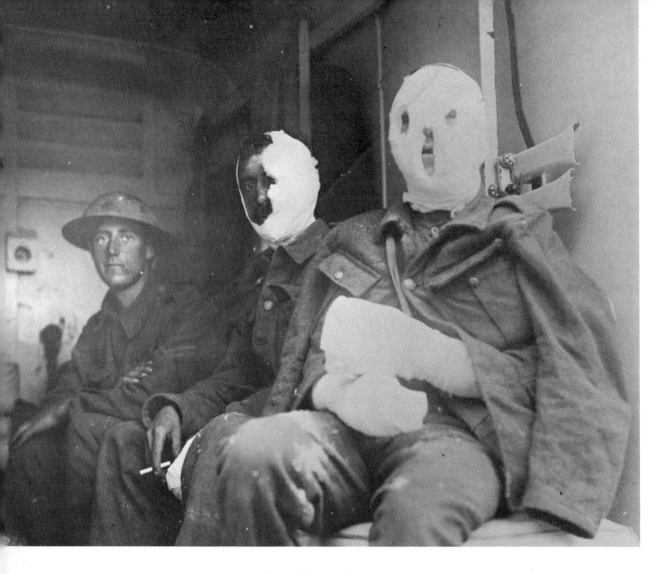

The fighting at Arleux

In the summer of 1917 the Canadian Corps had a Canadian commander. Byng, whose stock stood high after Vimy, left to command the Third Army. Sir Arthur Currie (knighted in June) succeeded Byng, and Maj.-Gen. A. C. Macdonell took over the 1st Division; by this time Maj.-Gen. H. E. Burstall had succeeded Turner in the 2nd. The general war situation for the Allies was anything but satisfactory. Russia was still in the war but no offensive could be expected from her after the March Revolution. The United States had entered the war but it would be 1918 before the Americans could make their presence felt in France. The French mutinies were tapering off under Pétain, but a period of convalescence for the French armies was still essential. Britain and the Dominions shouldered the main burden of the war, and Haig characteristically returned to the offensive. Lloyd George, who had no faith in Haig, grudgingly consented. The Prime Minister had been discredited by his backing of Nivelle. Haig's offensive, in Flanders, opened with the capture of Messines Ridge in early June; there was then a pause for further preparations. Meanwhile Haig directed the First Army, which included the Canadian Corps, to hold the Germans to their ground in the Arras sector, and thus away from Flanders. The First Army, in turn, directed the Corps on Lens as the main objective; but Currie objected. Lens was dominated by two heights and Currie proposed the capture of one of these—Hill 70—instead of Lens, for this would place the Germans at the Canadians' feet instead of the other way around.

Currie, Douglas Haig and Byng

Hill 70, before . . . and after the battle

The enemy was sensitive to the loss of Hill 70 and Currie turned that to his own advantage. He would seize the hill by means of a sudden blow and defend it strongly with infantry strongpoints based on machine-gun posts. He would then provoke enemy counter-attacks so that the Germans, drawn onto a killing-ground dominated by Canadian guns, would be destroyed; or, if they got through the concentrations of shells, they would be cut down by machine-gun fire. As had been the case at Vimy, the artillery plan became the framework for the battle as it did for every subsequent battle of the Canadian Corps.

The attack, by the 1st and 2nd Divisions, went in on 15 August after strong bombardment which included 3,500 drums, and a thousand shells, containing gas—a grim rejoinder to *flammenwerfer* (flame-thrower) techniques and mustard gas which the enemy had first introduced on this front in July. The infantry was supported by a rolling barrage just ahead, a "jumping barrage" in front of that, and, still further ahead, a barrage from the heavies moving from one strongpoint to another. Additionally 500 drums of blazing oil were projected at selected targets to build up a smoke screen and demoralize the defenders. Counter-battery fire, once again, subdued the enemy's retaliation. The hill was captured and then came the real ordeal—no fewer than twenty-one enemy counter-attacks, heavily pressed, between 15-18 August. The resolute enemy stormed the Canadian parapets repeatedly, hurling grenades into the trenches and sweeping them with scorching flame. There was the close fighting of shouting, lunging, wrestling men. The ordeal continued for four days and three nights of infernal noise, with quiet passages made horrible by the screams and groans of the wounded. But Currie and his team

Vimy Ridge in Canadian hands was always useful for observation

The Ridge from the air

Cavalry on the move to Passchendaele

of gunners had planned for counter-attacks; they broke down, one after the other, under artillery fire and infantry resistance from strongpoints, based on machine-guns, well dug in. It was the second great victory for the Corps. The hill did not change hands again during the war. Five enemy divisions had been met and smashed at a cost of 9,198 Canadian casualties against an estimated 20,000 for the Germans.*

To the north Haig's Flanders offensive had been pressed at the Third Battle of Ypres, better known as Passchendaele, which began on 31 July. The objective was the German submarine bases in the Belgian ports, but the four million shells that made up the preparatory bombardment rained down on reclaimed bogland to disrupt drainage patterns and create an obstacle in front of the attacking troops that doomed the offensive before it started. Tanks were tried but they were useless in the mud. The British butted forward on the pattern established at the Somme so that the line crept slowly towards Passchendaele Ridge at tremendous cost.** In the October rains the swamps submerged it. No army could winter on the present line and Haig had two alternatives: to withdraw to higher ground near Ypres; or to go on to seize the ridge. He would not relinquish ground that had cost so much blood; he would go on, then, and on 5 October he called for the troops who had given him the heights of Vimy and Hill 70 to break the deadlock at Passchendaele.

*Six more V.Cs. were won in this fighting around Lens: by Private Harry Brown of the 10th Battalion; Sergeant Frederick Hobson of the 20th Battalion; Private Michael James O'Rourke of the 7th Battalion; Major Okill Massey Learmonth of the 2nd Battalion; Sergeant-Major Robert Hanna of the 29th Battalion; and by Corporal Filip Konowal of the 47th.

**Lt.-Col. P. E. Bent, a Canadian serving with the British Army, won the V.C. on 1 October at Polygon Wood.

The shattered suburbs of Lens

The wastes of Passchendaele

By a strange irony of war—and an indication of war's futility—the front taken over by the Canadians was almost the same as that they had held before the gas attack in 1915. But veterans of Second Ypres could hardly recognize the place. It was as if a powerful flood had swept over the entire landscape snapping off the trees and destroying everything in its path; and as if, in their recession, the waters had left tons of sludge and slimy pools where had been farms and fields. Everywhere was the jetsam of war: light locomotives, sunk to their boilers; guns, axle-deep in mud, pointing grotesquely at the sky; and sprawling bodies that neither side could clear because of the continuous shelling. The swollen flanks of dead horses and mules shone in the rain; human remains lay on every side. Not every dead face was caked with mud. Some of the recently killed were white, others grey, green, black or decomposed. A disgusting odour of sickly, sweet-smelling death pressed heavily on the senses. On the higher ground, across the swamps, were the enemy defences based on machine-guns in concrete pillboxes, extremely strong.

79

Currie protested to Haig that the attack should not be made but his protests were unavailing; he put the cost at 16,000 men. He then insisted that ample time be given for preparations. Some of these concerned gunfire to screen the attacking troops. There had to be firm platforms for the guns to fire from for without them recoil would drive the pieces down so deeply that they would have to be constantly pried out and re-aimed. Others meant the construction of better roads to bring up reinforcements and supplies over the six-mile morass from Ypres.

The atrocious ground conditions at Passchendaele

The attack was scheduled for 26 October. The forward troops, sheltering in wet slimy shellholes, shivered under groundsheets throughout the night. At 5:40 A.M. they shed their heavy greatcoats to cut down weight and moved forward, blanketed by a cold wet mist, through the fetid mud. There were no less than seven curtains of fire to shield them fired by field guns, close in, then all the way through the various calibres to a leading curtain put down by the sixty-pounder guns. But because the guns were restricted to the newly-constructed platforms, the barrages were thin. The 3rd and 4th Divisions, fighting for three days under appalling conditions in mist and rain, plastered with mud, suffered 2,500 casualties and failed to reach their objectives; only discipline and comradeship had kept them going. But they did obtain a foothold on higher and drier ground. The value of this became apparent on 30 October during the next phase of the attack. That day the infantry struggled forward more than half a mile. The ground taken, however, cost 2,321 casualties.

Only a quarter of a mile still remained to secure the ridge but Currie made no bid as yet; he wanted fresh troops and replaced the exhausted divisions with the 1st and 2nd. This gave time to move both the heavy and field artilleries to better positions forward. Finally, at dawn on 6 November, the attack that marked the final phase went in. This time there was the old harmony between guns and assaulting troops as in the previous successful battles; in less than three hours the ridge was won. The terrible fighting for Passchendaele Ridge cost Canada 15,654 battle casualties—almost as many as Currie had predicted.

Things were quiet after Passchendaele. Prince Amoradhat of Siam, American, Portuguese and Roumanian officers visit the Canadian front, and a prisoner is interrogated

Haig's offensive was probably justified in May and even June. The parlous state of the French Army and the critical sinkings of ships by submarines were good reasons for it at that time. But by July, when the main offensive was launched, the French had recovered. The peak of the submarine crisis had also been reached and passed. The convoy system, introduced by Lloyd George, had achieved remarkable results. The first convoys sailed on 10 May, 1917, and they became the regular thing for Atlantic shipping. A convoy, far out at sea, was no more difficult to find than a single ship, and it was protected by destroyers. In convoys the rate of loss was one per cent; it had been twenty-five per cent before. Thus the offensive served no valid strategic ends; tactically, to drive a salient into a ridge four miles forward of the old line is of doubtful value. And from the point of view of sheer attrition the British lost more heavily than the Germans.

Canada remained aloof from the dissensions which inevitably arose. She had been given a job to do and had done it well; but at a grim price. In this Ypres Salient, and especially at Passchendaele, her sons had proved her right to call herself a nation.

Whether the Somme or Passchendaele was the most dreadful battle the Corps fought is a matter for conjecture.* It is certain that both were nightmares. For weeks, at Passchendaele, the dead lay buried amid the mud. In the spring, when the Newfoundlanders held the ridge, corpses rose out of the ooze and were cleared away. One morning stretcher parties blundered into a pair of bodies, perhaps symbolic of the whole campaign. One was Canadian, the other German, grappling still in death. They had fought desperately and, sucked into the swamp, had died in one another's arms. All efforts to part them failed and so a large grave was dug in which to bury the pitiful remains.

*Passchendaele brought the most V.Cs. for no fewer than nine were won:
by Private Thomas William Holmes of the 4th Canadian Mounted Rifles;
Captain Christopher Patrick John O'Kelly, the 52nd Battalion;
Lieutenant Robert Shankland, the 43rd Battalion; Private Cecil John Kinross,
49th Battalion; Lieutenant Hugh Mackenzie of the 7th Canadian Machine Gun
Company; Sergeant George Harry Mullin, Princess Patricia's; Major
George Randolph Pearkes of the 5th Canadian Mounted Rifles; Corporal
Colin Fraser Barron, 3rd Battalion; and by Private James Peter Robertson of the 27th.

Winter

Part Five:
The Battle of Cambrai, 1917

Courtesy of the National Gallery of Canada   *—Painted by Alfred Munnings*

CHARGE OF FLOWERDEW'S SQUADRON*

The Canadians might have been spared their ordeal at
Passchendaele if Sir Julian Byng had had his way. A staff
officer at Tank Corps Headquarters, who had watched the
tanks squandered during the early Passchendaele fighting,
protested the futility of using these battle-winning
machines in swamps. He suggested a large-scale raid by
massed tanks where the ground was favourable and Byng,

83

*This charge took place during the German offensives of 1918; it is typical, however, of the
cavalry fighting at Cambrai.

A sudden blow by tanks and artillery, firing without any preliminary bombardment, brought early success at Cambrai

whose Army was not embroiled in Flanders, adopted the idea for a proposed attack on Cambrai in September. He wanted his old Canadian Corps as the basic component of a force of tanks, guns, cavalry and infantry. But Haig had not yet recognized that the Flanders offensive was played out and he made no decision then on Byng's proposal. After the capture of Passchendaele Ridge, however, Haig sanctioned an attack in the chosen sector but the operation was transformed into an offensive by six divisions of Byng's Third Army.

The attack, led by almost four hundred tanks, was launched on 20 November. It completely surprised the Germans. The tanks were able to crush the wire and demolish strongpoints and so there had been no preparatory bombardment to alert the enemy; the artillery only fired when the tanks, followed by the infantry, began to move. The advance swept rapidly forward in a sector where the ground had not been torn up by long bombardment. The terrifying sight for the Germans, then, was that of a long line of tanks rumbling down upon them with wave after wave of infantry following close behind; and, simultaneously, the sudden flash of a thousand guns. The defenders in the forward zones surrendered or fled. Two defensive systems making up the forbidding Hindenburg Line were completely broken through on a six-mile front during the first day and the advance moved four miles forward.

Lieutenant Harcus Strachan, who won the V.C. during the Battle of
Cambrai, leads a squadron of the Fort Garry Horse

THE WAR OFFICE RECORDS CENTRE
Bourne Avenue, HAYES, Middlesex
Telephone: HAYES 3831, *ext.* 107

In any reply please quote:

63/130(WORC)   31st January, 1963

Sir,

I am directed to refer to your letter dated 23rd January, 1963 regarding the Royal Newfoundland Regiment and forward the following extracts from the available records.

1. After the engagements at YPRES and CAMBRAI in 1917, the Newfoundland Regiment was awarded the prefix "Royal". This is the only instance in which this was conferred <u>during</u> the Great War, though other regiments and Corps received the title <u>after</u> cessation of hostilities.

2. Two previous instances of the title "Royal" being conferred <u>during</u> hostilities are recorded.

3. These are:-

    (a) in 1695, after the siege of NAMUR the title "Royal Regiment of Foot of Ireland" was conferred on 18th Regiment of Foot by King William III for its magnificent courage in action. In addition the regiment was authorised to wear the badge of the Lion of Nassau. The Regiment was disbanded in 1922.

    (b) In 1885, in recognition of the gallant conduct of Princess Charlotte of Wales' (Berkshire) Regiment in the action at TOFREK, Queen Victoria approved of the regiment being thenceforth designated "Princess Charlotte of Wales' Royal Berkshire Regiment".

            I am, Sir,
                Your obedient Servant,

                    L. S. Kerr.

Colonel The Honourable Sir Leonard Outerbridge, CBE, DSO, CD, LL.D.,
The Royal Newfoundland Regiment,
St. John's,
NEWFOUNDLAND.

The Newfoundland Regiment's mascot, "Sable Chief"

On the Arras front, December 1917

The ringing of church bells in the British Isles to celebrate the victory was premature; success was in Byng's grasp but the reserves he needed to exploit the enemy's ruptured front were not available. These had been swallowed up at Passchendaele. From the second day onward the battle deteriorated into a race with German reinforcements. The first day's impetus was lost by the Third Army and at the end of the month the enemy mounted a powerful counter-attack in which, for the first time, he used infiltration tactics with which he had experimented on the moribund Russian front. The British were driven back and though they retained some of the ground won on 20 November, this was offset by the capture by the Germans of five miles of the original front south of Cambrai.

The Cambrai front, photographed in 1918

Cavalry and Infantry

At Cambrai the Canadian Cavalry Brigade, as it customarily did, fought with the British Cavalry Corps. Lieutenant Harcus Strachan, of the Fort Garry Horse, led a charge against an enemy battery, killing seven gunners with his sword. He won the V.C. for this exploit near the village of Masnières which the Newfoundland Regiment helped clear during the first day's advance. For its "magnificient and resolute determination" in holding ground near Masnières for eleven days, the battalion became "Royal" in February, 1918, an honour that was unique in the First World War. Private Thomas Ricketts of this regiment was to win the V.C. a month before the war ended.

The battle at Cambrai was important. It set the pattern for the German infiltration methods used during their offensives of 1918. The employment of massed tanks by the British paved the way for the great victories in the final months of the war; and the influence of this extended, even further, into the campaigns of the Second World War.

While Cambrai was being fought the Canadian Corps wintered on the Arras front

Part Six:
In Canada

Courtesy of the National Gallery of Canada   —Painted by Mabel May

WOMEN MAKING SHELLS

The raising of reinforcements in Canada caused no serious
problem for the first eighteen months of the war. Men still came
forward as volunteers though there was now a clear-eyed
realization of what that would mean. There was a determination
to see the war through to a successful conclusion and to spare
nothing that would make it possible. Canada had done much
but she was, in Sir Robert Borden's words, "not only prepared"
but "willing to do something more."

On New Year's Day, 1916, Borden pledged half a million men in uniform and that meant the doubling of the forces' present strength. Such a formidable goal, it seems clear now, was prompted by the Prime Minister's determination to use a good war record by Canada as a passport to full autonomy. There had been no request from Britain for a force of such a size, but, said Borden, "It can hardly be expected that we shall put 400,000 or 500,000 men in the field and willingly accept the position of having no more voice and receiving no more consideration than if we were toy automata."

Women undertook clerical work formerly performed by men

The Princess Patricia presents colours to the P.P.C.L.I., the battalion which bears her name

At home, women replaced men in many spheres

By the early summer of 1916 the needs of industry and agriculture, which had expanded greatly under the stimulus of war, brought increasing demands on manpower; the recruiting situation began to deteriorate. Then came the Somme, with its enormous toll, and at the end of the year the impossibility of placing even the 5th Division in the field—let alone half a million men—had become apparent.

The appetite of the Western Front for shells

In January, 1917, the British asked for the commitment of the 5th Division but the difficulties of reinforcing five divisions meant that it stayed in England; early in 1918 it was broken up for reinforcements. By May, 1917, Borden had made up his mind that the voluntary system must give way to compulsory military service. In London, the Canadian Prime Minister had called for "full recognition of the Dominions as autonomous nations of an Imperial Commonwealth" and the name "Commonwealth" instead of "Empire" had been adopted. He was convinced that the great step forward to full autonomy would be won for Canada on the field of battle. Canada's effort, therefore, must not flag or falter even if there had to be conscription to maintain the strength of the Canadian Corps—a formation that was now recognized as a powerful national force.

In June, 1917, Borden introduced his Military Service Bill. It split the country and, at the General Election of 1917, Sir Robert appealed to the electorate as the head of a Union Government. In that election, women, for the first time, were given the vote. Nursing sisters, who had done much in the war, were all enfranchised, as were the wives, widows, mothers, sisters and daughters of persons, male or female, living or dead, who were serving or who had served outside Canada in the Canadian or British forces; finally, in 1918, the government granted a full and equal franchise to all women.

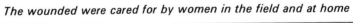

The wounded were cared for by women in the field and at home

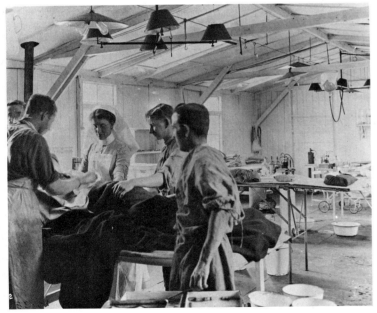

They worked in factories, drove ambulances and ran canteens

The work of women in the war deserves special notice. Not only did they serve overseas as nursing sisters and as drivers; they ran canteens and clubs and freed men from office tasks. In all, 2,400 nurses went overseas. More than five hundred helped staff hospitals in Canada. Of those abroad, some lost their lives; other earned decorations for valour and Red Cross Medals.

Their contribution at home was always large. Voluntary societies worked devotedly in providing comforts for the troops, medical supplies, ambulances and equipment of a hundred sorts; of them, the Imperial Order of the Daughters of the Empire (the largest single organization) founded and equipped a Red Cross hospital in London. As many as 20,000 women were employed in making shells and aircraft; thousands more worked on farms. The economic life was largely sustained by women. They worked long hours in the civil service, in banks and and insurance firms. Over ten thousand, without previous training, entered business life. Women, it has been truly said, provided much more than sympathy in the First World War.

Comforts for the troops

As the result of the election of 1917 a Union Government was elected with a majority of 71. The Liberals won only 82 seats of which 62 were in Quebec, where, when the Military Service Act was enforced, there were disorders. Conscription produced the reinforcements required but at the price of endangering national unity.

The Military Service Act, at least, was selective. It directed men, not only to the army, but to agriculture and industry as well and this was important. The products of the Canadian farmer were a large factor in any successful ending to the war. More than two billion dollars worth of farm products, both agricultural and animal, were shipped abroad during the war years, most of them to Britain. In the two pre-war years the average yearly value of Canada's exports of butter, cheese, eggs, oats and wheat was $118,000,000; for 1918 alone the export was $455,000,000. Exports of beef and pork steadily increased as the war wore on; beef exports were 42,000,000 pounds greater in 1918 than in 1917, and pork went up by 23,000,000 pounds in the same year. And there were comparable increases in minerals, lumber, and fish.

Railway maintenance, performed by women

Canadian manufacturing industries, however, showed the
most startling development. The transformation of Canada from a
basically agricultural society to one greatly industrialized
really began during the First World War. German exports to
Canada, which were considerable, ceased with the outbreak of
war and Canadian production replaced them to a large extent.
The prime impetus, however, came with the manufacture of
munitions. In 1914 no munitions of any importance were
made in Canada; a month after the outbreak of the war, however,
Colonel Hughes—with remarkable foresight—recognized
Canada's capacity to do so and set up a Shell Committee.
In January, 1915, fifty Canadian manufacturers, large and small,
were engaged in shell production for the British Government.
The tide swelled, and, by March, 200 factories had been enrolled
to fill contracts worth $80,000,000, including those for fuses,
an extremely skilled operation. In mid-1915 no less than
247 factories, in 78 towns and cities and employing between
60,000 and 70,000, were engaged; and in 1918, 300,000 men
and women found employment in these and other factories.

97

Some of the guns captured by Canadians during "The Hundred Days"

Already for the year 1915-1916, Canada exported $250,000,000 of manufactures, four times the 1914 figure, and certain industries, subsidiary to shellmaking and which would have a permanent effect in developing the resources of the country, had been established. The total exports of manufactures for the war period amounted to more than a billion dollars.

In the four years preceding the war, the total exports of Canada had been only $1,484,743,600 against imports of $2,318,643,002. During the four-year war period, however, imports of $2,965,497,837 were outweighed by exports amounting to $4,335,549,319—leaving a balance of some $1,370,000,000 in Canada's favour.

At the outbreak of hostilities Canada was a debtor nation as, in fact, she had been since Confederation but, with the demands created by war, the position changed dramatically.

Weapons multiplied, creating heavy demands for ammunition

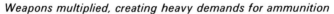

Part Seven:
The Final Year

Courtesy of the National Gallery of Canada —*Painted by Alfred Bastien*

OVER THE TOP on the way to the Drocourt-Quéant Line

At the beginning of 1918 Germany was stronger than the Allies on the Western Front. The Bolsheviks had seized power in Russia and thus a new ideology, that would have great future significance, was loose. In December, 1917, they signed an armistice with Germany. This enabled the Germans to transfer divisions from east to west. Despite the arrival of American troops in Europe, the Allies would not achieve numerical superiority until the middle of the year.

Lloyd George, who was appalled at the cost of Passchendaele, withheld from France the bulk of the reinforcements that Haig demanded. To meet the shortage, Haig reduced the number of battalions in his infantry brigades from four to three and used the troops of the surplus battalion to bring the others up to strength. There were thus fewer British battalions, and weaker

99

The Victoria Cross

brigades, to hold the front. Currie was expected to conform but he refused to tamper with a proved machine. Nor did he want the two additional divisions that the reorganization would bring, for that would mean a Canadian Army of two corps; British staff officers would be required and the present Canadian homogeneity—so laboriously fostered—would be destroyed. Instead, Currie augmented each of the forty-eight battalions of the Canadian Corps by one hundred men, thus increasing their fighting strength without any increase in the staffs of higher formations. The 5th Division, in England, was broken up for this. Thus a stronger Corps—not a weaker—embarked upon the war's last year.

On 21 March the Germans, with no preparatory bombardment, suddenly struck at two British armies.* Ludendorff's tactics, first tried at Cambrai, were novel. Acting on the principle of "infiltration," light probing forces of storm troops would find spots weakened by artillery fire and then push deep. Other troops, following closely, would widen the breaches and thrust still deeper into the defensive lines. The avoidance of tough pockets of resistance, and thus heavy casualties, was obviously better than butting obstinately against defences all along the front. That night, by use of infiltration tactics, they had broken clean through the Fifth Army's front but on 5 April they were finally held short of Amiens. The Canadian Cavalry Brigade, fighting both as cavalry and as infantry (dismounted) helped bring about this result. In a spirited action it cleared the enemy out of Moreuil Wood, a commanding position on the right bank of the Avre, only twelve miles southeast of Amiens. Lieutenant G. M. Flowerdew, of Lord Strathcona's Horse, won the V.C. while leading, under heavy fire, a charge against the enemy during this period. The firepower and mobility of the armoured cars of the 1st Canadian Motor Machine Gun Brigade also played an effective part in covering the withdrawal of the infantry and filling dangerous gaps. The Allies, badly shaken by this first offensive, appointed a Frenchman to co-ordinate the French and British armies. At the beginning of April Marshal Foch became co-ordinator and then Commander-in-Chief of all the Allied forces.

*That day 2nd Lt. Edmund DeWind, a Canadian serving with the British, won the V.C.

The War Lords of Germany: Hindenburg and Ludendorff with the Kaiser (centre)

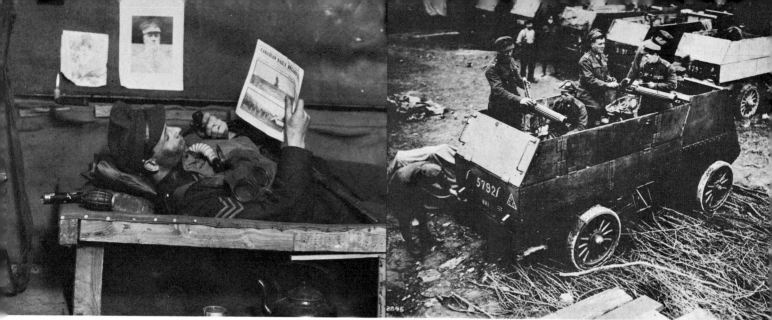

Before "The Hundred Days"

Motor machine-guns

Baulked at Amiens, with no wedge driven between the British and French, the Germans struck in Flanders for the Channel ports. The offensive swept away the gains of Passchendaele, which had cost so much, but Haig conducted the defence with skill; the German drive was stopped at Hazebrouck. A third offensive, to draw reserves from Flanders, went in against the French and though the Germans reached the Marne they got no further. On 9 June they attempted to widen this southern salient but again were checked. Then, in July, the Germans mounted their last offensive, once more in Champagne, across the Marne.

By now the Americans had arrived in force and the Allies had superior numbers. The time had come, Foch realized, for a counter-blow which he delivered; by 7 August the Germans had been forced back, not only from the Marne, but behind the River Vesle. With that the initiative on the Western Front passed from the Germans to the Allies.

A time of preparation: infantry-tank co-operation,

building up supplies

A war artist at work

The Canadian Corps, as such, had taken no part in these offensives. When the Germans first struck, Haig had ordered the Canadians, piecemeal by divisions, to shore up the crumbling British front. Currie protested the break-up of his Corps, pointing out that its efficiency and high morale were due to its cohesion under Canadian leadership; the War Office upheld him. The lessons of the great victories at Vimy, Hill 70 and Passchendaele had not been lost in London where it was recognized that the past policy of keeping the Corps together had produced tremendous results. Only the 2nd Division, which had already been detached and was embroiled in the fighting, fought with the British until July when the Corps was again complete. Currie held sixteen miles of front, including Hill 70 and Vimy Ridge, throughout the German offensives and ceded not one inch of ground. These were important features for behind them lay the only collieries remaining to the French in northern France as well as key centres of communication. Despite huge pockets carved out by the Germans north and south of the Canadian line, the Corps stood firm. Its attitude was aggressive; the infantry carried out numerous raids* and patrols and firmly repelled enemy reprisals.

Not only that; Currie used this relatively quiet period to re-organize the Canadian Corps and to train it for the open warfare he envisaged when the striking-power of the enemy had died away. An example of this is his centralization of machine-gun troops; in future they were to be regarded as a distinctive arm, with tactics of their own. Six months later, the British followed his example.

The Germans, tactically, had had success; strategically, they had lost the war. They had scored no decisive victory and the numerical superiority of their opponents was increasing. The huge salients they carved in the Allied front meant longer lines to hold. Badly attenuated, the enemy lay wide open for counter-strokes.

*Two V.Cs. were won during this period by Lieutenant G. B. McKean of the 14th Battalion; and by Corporal Joseph Kaeble of the 22nd Battalion.

Positioning the heavies

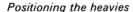

By the time the German offensives had ended, the Canadians fielded a strong, fresh, well-trained and well-organized corps, ready to play an important part in the fighting that lay ahead. The months spent on the Lens-Arras front had not been wasted.

Dominion Day was especially well celebrated that year. The Corps was in reserve. On that day the 2nd Division returned and fifty thousand Canadians assembled for sports at Tincques, fourteen miles west of Arras. A stadium had been knocked together by the engineers, complete with a platform for distinguished guests. Sir Robert Borden, General John J. Pershing (Commander-in-Chief, American Expeditionary Forces) and the Duke of Connaught all attended. There were marquees for refreshments and an open-air theatre where the "Dumbells" gave continuous performances. Planes hovered overhead to protect the Corps from enemy bombing. That night the "Volatiles", the concert party of the 1st Division, presented its revue, "Take a Chance". Sir Robert Borden inspected units of the Corps next day, and on the 6th, the 3rd Brigade, which had three Scottish battalions, played host to Highland regiments of the British Army. The week was peacetime soldiering, brass and weapons twinkling in the sun, flags, massed bands and stirring music; the Highland Gathering wound it up in proper style with Highland games, skirling pipe bands, and the march of pipes and drums. Morale was extremely high when on 15 July the Corps came out of reserve and relieved the British XVIIth Corps in the line.

Currie with Pershing, the American C-in-C

Haig proposed a blow at Amiens to give a margin of safety around the town and Foch agreed. He placed the French First Army at Haig's disposal to act on the right of the British Fourth to which the Canadian Corps would go. Haig decided to use the methods of Cambrai for the battle, in the interests of surprise.

For Amiens it was always more important to conceal from the enemy the intentions of the Canadian Corps than any other formation. "Regarding them as storm troops", wrote Sir

Sir Douglas Haig congratulates the Canadians after the victory at Amiens

Basil Liddell Hart, the eminent British military historian, ''the enemy tended to greet their appearance as an omen of a coming attack.'' Currie, therefore, prepared a mock attack on the Arras front to delude the enemy and then, at the last possible moment before the real attack which was scheduled for 8 August, moved the Corps south to Amiens by night.
The frontage of the forthcoming battle was fourteen miles with the French in the southern half; the Fourth Army named two corps for the assault, the Canadians on the right and the Australians on the left, with the British IIIrd Corps acting as flank-guard on the extreme left. ''The Corps was used as the spear-head'', said Arthur Currie, ''the centre of the attack. All other troops taking part in the battle...conformed to the movement of the Canadian Corps. We made the plan; we set the time and pace in that battle.''

The Battle of Amiens began an hour before dawn on 8 August. Surprise was total. More than two thousand guns suddenly flashed out in barrage and counter-battery tasks to usher in the day with an earlier, explosive dawn, while 420 tanks, closely followed by the infantry, surged forward over ground that was heavily shrouded in mist. German machine-gunners found few targets as the tanks, accompanied by determined men, crashed through their positions. The enemy artillery, which might have been counted on to break up the attack despite the fog, had been effectively neutralized by counter-battery fire; batteries were quickly overrun, many of them without having fired a shot. In what was then open warfare, massed cavalry and light ''whippet'' tanks swept ahead to exploit success. On that first victorious day, ''The Black Day of the German Army,'' as the enemy termed it, the Canadians gained eight miles, the Australians seven, the French five and the British two. The Germans lost 27,000 men and 400 guns as well as mortars and machine-guns in their hundreds; the Canadian Corps alone captured 5,033 prisoners and 161 guns. Against this, the Fourth Army's casualties totalled 9,000—about 4,000 for the Corps.

French

Field guns in the Canadian War Museum

German

After Amiens

Greater than this material loss was the moral effect that Amiens had on the German Army. This battle was the decisive engagement of the First World War. But though it had been the most brilliant success ever gained on the Allied side during the war, its decisive character did not arise from the extent of the victory or its strategic value. It was not even the turning point of the war; the course of the campaign had already been reversed when the French wrested the initiative out of German hands a month before. What Amiens did was to undermine the morale of the German Supreme Command.

Hotchkiss and Lewis machine-guns in the Canadian War Museum

105

The decline in German fighting power disturbed Ludendorff most. He had never admitted before, even to himself, that endurance had begun to crack. Strong divisions from the overseas Dominions had now flung the fact in his face. They had attacked with "squadrons of tanks, but otherwise in no great superiority," and yet "six or seven divisions, which could certainly be described as battle-worthy, had been completely broken." Now, Ludendorff was forced to acknowledge, the German war machine was "no longer efficient."

The Battle of Amiens continued until 11 August but the later gains were small. It was difficult for the attackers to adjust to fluid, mobile conditions after years of static warfare; and the Germans, alarmed, rushed up eighteen divisions to seal this broken front. In any case the advance soon reached the formidable trench-lines of the old Somme battlefield of 1916 and to tackle those would mean the costly pattern of trench warfare once again. After the exhilaration of the recent battle, Currie could not stomach that and, at his instigation, the fighting was broken off.*

A British historian, A. J. P. Taylor, has recorded that after Amiens, "Foch wanted to press the attack in the old frontal way. Haig at first agreed; then was persuaded by his subordinate commanders to stop whenever the enemy proved obstinate. In this accidental way, Foch and Haig stumbled unwillingly on a new and wiser method—to attack at weak points, not at strong ones; they quickly took the credit for it." The initiative came from Currie who had listened to the protests of his Counter Battery Staff Officer, Lieut.-Colonel A. G. L. McNaughton, who was to command the First Canadian Army in the Second World War.

Instead of butting up against the Somme defences, Currie proposed an attack in a new sector—the thrust which he had prepared as the cover-plan for Amiens and which could be

*Ten V.Cs. were earned in the Amiens battle: by Lieutenant Jean Brillant of the 22nd Battalion; Lieutenant J. E. Tait of the 78th; Corporal H. J. Good and Private J. B. Croak, both of the 13th Battalion; Corporal H. G. B. Miner of the 58th; Corporal Alexander Brereton and Corporal F. G. Coppins, both of the 8th Battalion; Sergeant R. L. Zengel of the 5th; Private Thomas Dinesen of the 42nd Battalion; and Sergeant Robert Spall of the P.P.C.L.I.

Captured guns

Bourlon, on the way to Cambrai

Major Georges Vanier, a future Governor-General of Canada, who lost his right leg in the fighting for the Fresnes-Rouvroy Line

mounted quickly. This, striking out from Arras, would be aimed at Cambrai, the hub of the German defensive system on the British front. There were very strong defences between these two places: the old British trenches, lost in March 1918, near Monchy-le-Preux; beyond, the old German front line; behind that, the Fresnes-Rouvroy Line; east of that, the Drocourt-Quéant Line which, an extension of the Hindenburg Line, was deemed by the Germans to be impregnable; and, between that and Cambrai, the Canal du Nord which formed a major obstacle. On 14 August, Haig ordered the First Army, to which the Canadian Corps would go, to strike out from Arras; the attack was co-ordinated with that of the Third Army, on the right.

Currie opened the Battle of the Scarpe, part of Second Arras, on 26 August at the unusually early hour of 3 A.M. to gain surprise. The Canadian Corps, spearhead of the Second Army, seized Monchy and the ground a thousand yards behind it (including both the old British and German trench-lines) by nightfall. Lieutenant C. S. Rutherford of the 5th Canadian Mounted Rifles, who captured 70 prisoners and knocked out several machine-guns single-handed, won the V.C. at Monchy.

There was no pause. Currie's orders for the 27th directed the Corps on the Fresnes-Rouvroy Line. Resistance was bitter, and it was not before the 28th that the line was pierced. Lieutenant-Colonel W. H. Clark-Kennedy, who commanded the 24th Battalion, earned a V.C. for his gallant leadership despite a serious wound. By now the Canadians had thrust five miles forward since the 26th and captured more than 3,000 prisoners, fifty pieces of artillery and five hundred machine-guns. But the main task—the extension of the Hindenburg Line between Drocourt and Quéant—lay ahead.

The formidable D-Q Line

It would be folly to attack such a formidable obstacle before the Corps was fully ready and Currie asked for, and obtained, a respite until 2 September. The intervening days were well spent by the heavy artillery in wire-cutting and counter-battery operations but so dense was the wire that not all of it could be cut. Tanks, therefore, would be used to roll paths for the assaulting infantry.

At dawn on the 2nd, tanks and infantry surged forward behind a strong barrage to tackle the enemy's main defensive line on the Western Front; by nightfall it was in Canadian hands on a frontage of seven thousand yards. Veterans will remember the exposed slopes and crest of Mont Dury—swept by storms of machine-gun bullets—which they captured; there were many dead and wounded men.* The fighting between 1-3 September cost Canada 5,500 casualties of all types. Although the enemy concealed his losses, seven divisions are known to have been overcome; 6,000 prisoners were taken.

The Canadian victory was significant. Hindenburg admitted, "On September 2 a fresh hostile attack overran our lines once and for all on the great Arras-Cambrai road and compelled us to bring the whole front back to the Siegfried [Hindenburg] Line. For the sake of economizing men we simultaneously evacuated the salient north of the Lys which bulged out beyond Mount Kemmel and Merville." In other words, the wedge that the Canadians had driven in threatened to open a flank that would turn the Hindenburg system; thus the Germans withdrew behind the Hindenburg defences as far south as the Aisne and also in Flanders and, by doing so, relinquished all their gains from offensives earlier in the year. By obviating the fighting which other Allied formations would have had to reach the Line, the Canadian action had materially shortened the war.

That was not all. Currie's battle on 2 September forced the Germans to adopt extreme measures. Labour was diverted for new defences, the Hermann Line, farther back. All military material not required for immediate use was removed from the

*There were no less than seven V.Cs. that day: Lieutenant-Colonel C. W. Peck and Lance-Corporal W. H. Metcalf of the 16th Battalion; Captain B. S. Hutcheson, a medical officer attached to the 75th Battalion; Sergeant A. G. Knight of the 10th Battalion; Private C. J. P. Nunney of the 38th Battalion; Private W. L. Rayfield of the 7th Battalion; and Private J. F. Young of the 87th Battalion.

Steam tractors hauling heavy naval guns

region west of that line, railways and roads demolished, and coal mines wrecked. A more distant line, the Antwerp-Meuse, was reconnoitred. The fortresses of Alsace-Lorraine were put into a state of defence. And, to avoid capture, supplies from Germany were ordered to be cut down to the bare essentials. Well might Currie wonder in his diary on 3 September "whether our victory of yesterday or of August 8th" was greater; he was "inclined to think yesterday's was."

There was a pause after 2 September to permit other Allied forces to come up to the Hindenburg defences. On 3 September Marshal Foch outlined his plans. Of three British Armies, the First faced the Canal du Nord; the Third and Fourth were approaching the Hindenburg Line. So that the enemy would not mass all his reserves against them, Foch ordered a general offensive all along the front. It would consist of four powerful blows: by the three British armies against Cambrai and St. Quentin; by the French, in the centre, beyond the Aisne; by the Americans, farther south at St. Mihiel, later combining with the French towards Mézières; and, in the north, by the British Second Army, with the Belgians, towards Ghent and Bruges. These attacks, closely co-related, hustled the Germans to defeat.

The Canadian Corps played a conspicuous part in the final victory. As the striking force of the First Army, it forced the formidable barrier of the Canal du Nord on 27 September and by so doing afforded flank protection to the Third Army, immediately to the south, which on the same day, breached the Hindenburg Line southwest of Cambrai. All this helped the Fourth Army, south of the Third, to bore through the Hindenburg defences north of St. Quentin two days later and burst into the open country three miles beyond.

At the Canal du Nord, Currie was faced with the canal itself, which was about a hundred feet across, and by marshes on both sides of it which had been extensively flooded to widen the obstacle. The defences consisted of machine-gun posts close to the water and, about a mile farther back, the Marquion Line. On a lofty hill behind this line reared Bourlon Wood, and between the wood and Cambrai was yet another defensive line, the Marcoing system. A frontal attack would be suicidal because of the flooded ground and the successive defences. Currie chose instead to tackle a stretch to the south where, through construction work having been halted by the outbreak of war, the canal was dry.

Through the one-and-a-half-mile funnel of the dry gap Currie proposed to pass 50,000 men, guns, tanks, and transport and,

109

The dry section of the Canal du Nord

after reaching the farther bank, to spread them out fanwise
to the north and east, enveloping the defences as they went.
It was a daring conception calling for skilful leadership and
strict discipline; Byng described it as "the most difficult
operation that has yet been tried in the war." The danger will be
apparent. If the German artillery should ever become alert to
the congestion in the narrow avenue of assault there would
be disaster. Yet against that risk was the certainty, in a frontal
assault, of extremely heavy casualties still without assurance
of success.

By midnight on 26-27 September the troops for the attack had
assembled opposite the dry section of the canal, huddled
together for warmth, and for the most part in the open. Apart
from light showers, the rain that threatened held off and the
skies cleared. The men, as the slow night waned, anxiously
watched the brightening eastern sky. Suddenly, with intense,
pulsating light—followed by the thunder of the guns—the
opening barrage flashed out, shocking the men to action.
The answering fire fell elsewhere and it was not before the
morning was well advanced that the enemy became alive to his
danger and subjected the dry bed of the canal to a violent
bombardment. By that time the initial waves of troops were
well over and fanning out from the bridgehead, but the
follow-up troops inevitably suffered.

Nevertheless, the results of the first day justified Currie's
generalship. At relatively light cost he had the line of the
Canal du Nord, the Marquion Line and Bourlon Wood—the key
to Cambrai and therefore the essential objective—by nightfall.

The successful results of 27 September were not matched on the succeeding days. The enemy, sensitive to the loss of Cambrai and the railways converging on it (which would threaten their communications both north and south), poured in reinforcements. German strength facing the Corps grew from four divisions on 27 September to ten by 1 October, as well as thirteen Marksmen Machine-Gun Companies that could offer sturdy resistance under condition of open warfare. Parts of the Marcoing Line fell on 28 September but afterwards progress became extremely slow. The 29th was a day of exhausting probing that proved costly and yielded little, and yet the pressure was still maintained until the enemy should crack. Next day, however, a general attack broke down under murderous machine-gun fire and fierce counter-attacks; the story was the same when the assault was renewed on 1 October. That night, in view of the bone-weariness of his troops, Currie broke off the action.

What was not immediately apparent was that the Germans were now fought out. The Canadian thrust, combined with those by the Third and Fourth Armies to the south, had so used up the German reserves that the enemy was at present incapable of any further major resistance.

The Canadian Corps, refreshed by a week's rest, returned to the attack on the night 8-9 October. The general plan was to seize the Escaut bridges leading into Cambrai and then, avoiding house-to-house fighting, to cut the town off from the north. At the same time the British XVIIth Corps would carry out similar operations to the south. XVIIth Corps failed to take a preliminary objective and the Canadians attacked alone.

Their assault, in the middle of a pitch-black squally night, caught the enemy preparing to withdraw. The bridges were reached with almost ridiculous ease. Before dawn patrols had pushed into Cambrai to find it deserted except for demolition parties who were busily engaged in setting the town ablaze.*
By 8:30 A.M. the whole place was in Canadian hands and the Corps pushed on to free the district to the north, which it completed as far as the line of the Canal de la Sensée by 11 October.

Since 26 August the Corps head fought forward twenty-three miles through the backbone of the German defensive system. German losses, never published, included 19,000 prisoners

Ruined Cambrai

*There were eight Canadian V.Cs. in the fighting from the Canal du Nord to Cambrai: Lieutenant G. T. Lyall of the 102nd Battalion; Lieutenant S. L. Honey of the 78th; Lieutenant G. F. Kerr of the 3rd Battalion; Lieutenant M. F. Gregg of the R.C.R.; Captain John MacGregor of the 2nd C.M.R.; Sergeant William Merrifield of the 4th Battalion; Captain C. N. Mitchell of the 4th Battalion, Canadian Engineers; and Lieutenant W. L. Algie of the 20th Battalion.

as well as 300 guns and 2,000 machine-guns. These gains were, as Currie said, largely due to "iron discipline" and to all the components of the Corps working smoothly together in the over-all machine.

Meanwhile, on 9 October—the day the Canadian Corps captured Cambrai—the Canadian Cavalry Brigade had taken part in the last cavalry action of the war.

The British Cavalry Corps was given the task of sweeping away strong centres of resistance which slowed the advance of Fourth Army. In an attack by the 3rd Cavalry Division, the Fort Garry Horse, with four machine-guns and a battery of R.C.H.A., led the Canadian brigade (now commanded by Brig.-Gen. R. W. Paterson, a Canadian, who had replaced Seely) with Lord Strathcona's Horse on the left flank. A charge by the Strathcona's cleared one enemy rearguard from the village of Clary while the Fort Garrys tackled another in Gattigny Wood. With the help of South African infantry, the wood was cleared, yielding 200 prisoners, one howitzer and forty machine-guns.

Later in the day a squadron of the Royal Canadian Dragoons, assisted by dismounted Fort Garry troops and the guns of the R.C.H.A. Brigade, cleared Reumont of the enemy. The Dragoons and the Strathconas moved forward to cut the enemy's line in the vicinity of Le Cateau.

In all, the Cavalry Brigade advanced eight miles on a three-mile front. It captured more than 400 prisoners and materially aided the infantry's progress.

After Cambrai, the First Army directed the Canadian Corps on Valenciennes. On 17 October the Corps began the march and at first, apart from demolitions, the Germans did little to obstruct it. On the 16th Ludendorff had ordered his troops back to the Hermann Line, part of which was based on Valenciennes. For four days the Corps marched steadily along the *pavé* roads, following up the retreating Germans. They liberated the town of Denain and many villages to the acclaim of cheering French civilians, though some, it was remarked, were weeping.

When the Canadians entered, Cambrai was ablaze

On the 21st the Germans began to show their teeth. The Corps was approaching Valenciennes and it became more and more apparent that the enemy would have to be driven out by force. The town, as a key point in the Hermann Line, had been well chosen, for the only approaches were dominated by a heavily defended hill, Mont Houy. Of five German divisions holding Valenciennes, three were on or near Mont Houy.

At the Battle of Valenciennes, fought on 1 November, the Corps won its most economical victory of the war. At the instigation of Brig.-Gen. A. G. L. McNaughton, the young commander of the Corps Heavy Artillery, the guns did what he had always felt they had the power to do—to render the enemy impotent while the Canadain infantrymen were in the greatest danger and give them the opportunity to close with the bayonet. He planned such heavy barrages that one brigade advanced virtually unmolested against three divisions (with two others in reserve) and seized Mont Houy. Shells smothered the enemy positions in frontal, oblique, enfilade and reverse barrages as well as in solid blocks of fixed bombardment. Almost as much ammunition (2,149 tons) was expended by the Canadians as had been fired by both sides throughout the whole of the South African War (2,800 tons). There had been nothing like this bombardment in the whole history of war for intensity. Eight hundred enemy dead were counted in the Mont Houy area alone. One thousand, eight hundred Germans—shocked and dazed—surrendered. Against those figures, Canadian casualties amounted to only eighty killed and three hundred wounded—extremely few by the bloody yardstick of the First World War. The last Canadian V.C. of the war was won at Valenciennes, by Sergeant Hugh Cairns of the 46th Battalion for his conspicuous bravery in clearing machine-gun posts and field guns from the path of his platoon. Having jolted the enemy out of the Hermann Line by the decisive use of artillery, the triumphant Canadians swept on to Mons.

By this time the German nation and its allies had been collapsing for a month. On 26 September the Americans had

Motor machine-guns enter Mons

Welcome in Mons

*The Prince of Wales,
attached to the Canadian Corps,
enters liberated Denain*

opened the Meuse-Argonne battle on the British right which
drew-off German reserves to the south. The British Second Army
and the Belgians had advanced in Flanders to recover Messines
and Passchendaele and plough forward before being halted
by mud and war-torn ground. And that same month a British
offensive in Syria smashed the Turks. At the end of September,
Bulgaria capitulated as the result of the Salonika campaign,
which had followed the Dardanelles venture.

On 4 October both Germany and Austria-Hungary asked
President Wilson of the United States for armistice negotiations
and on the 24th Wilson abandoned the concept of a
negotiated armistice for what was virtually unconditional
surrender. Even that could not be avoided.

During the night 10-11 November the Canadians entered
Mons, the scene of the first engagement between British and
German troops in 1914. Thus the British, through the Canadian
Corps which had always fought as part of British armies,
were back where they had been at the start of the war. Was it
for this that countless casualties had been endured? The war
had been a foul experience and the return long and arduous.
Then, on 11 November at eleven o'clock, the Armistice came
into effect and hostilities ceased. It was the end of the road.

Part Eight:
After the Armistice

Courtesy of the National Gallery of Canada

—Painted by George A. Reid

ARMISTICE DAY, TORONTO

On 11 November the Allied peoples began a frenzy of rejoicing.
Work stopped and dancing crowds blocked the streets.
In London, Canadian soldiers lit a bonfire at the foot of Nelson's
column in Trafalgar Square, the marks of which can still be seen.
The celebrations went on, increasingly riotous, until in the end
police cleared the streets.

Currie, escorted by British 5th Lancers (all of whom had
served at Mons in 1914), entered Mons during the afternoon of
the 11th. The narrow streets were thronged with wildly
cheering people.

Bands played in the densely packed *Grande Place*. Soldiers

115

Currie takes the salute in Mons

Foch signs the Armistice

wore red carnations in their caps. The Canadian commander and his escort clattered across the rough cobblestones, dismounted, and met the gathered dignitaries of Mons. The Mayor delivered an address of welcome, punctuated at every pause by shouts of *Vive les braves Canadiens!* Currie replied, his "authoritative voice clear, vigorous, and sincere"; he presented to the city the Canadian Corps' flag. Selected contingents of the Corps then marched past to *La Brabançonne,* the Belgian national anthem, and at the conclusion of the march past Currie was conducted to the City Hall. There he signed the Gold Book of Remembrance.

The Canadians spent a week at Mons where they were fêted and acclaimed. The *Place de la Bavarie,* where Canadian troops first entered, was renamed the *Place du Canada.* King Albert of the Belgians made a state entry and congratulated Currie on his troops, "unsurpassed by any Corps in Europe." And over the town, from music borrowed from a regimental band, the carillon in the ancient belfry tower pealed out Canada's national airs.

The Armistice was signed in a train which stood in the Forêt de Compiègne

116

Borden addresses troops

Time would be required to bring back all the overseas troops. It was a year before repatriation and demobilization could be completed. Currie learned at Mons that his men, as an honour they had well earned, were to march to the Rhineland as part of General Plumer's Second Army which would form the British Army of Occupation. The Corps provided two divisions, a sixth of the total occupation force. On Sunday, 17 November, thanksgiving services were held and the dead remembered; next day the 1st and 2nd Divisions crossed the outpost lines and began the long journey to the Rhine with the 1st leading the march to Cologne and the 2nd to Bonn.

The Armistice had provided for the occupation by Allied troops of the left bank of the Rhine together with bridgeheads, each with a radius of thirty kilometres, at the principal crossing places on the other bank. The British would hold one bridgehead in the Cologne area which would incorporate the bridges at both Cologne and Bonn. It was arranged that Sir Herbert Plumer would take the salute at the Cologne crossing; at Bonn the distinction was accorded to Sir Arthur Currie.

"Putting the tin hat on it"

Currie takes the salute at Bonn

On 12 December, British cavalry units crossed into Bonn under the protection of batteries of the Canadian Corps Heavy Artillery deployed to cover the bridge and other vital points. Next day Currie, from a dais by the iron bridge rail, witnessed the crossing of Canada's remarkable infantry in drenching rain.

Occupation duty lasted until early in February when the troops returned to Belgium. A number of soldiers, both in Belgium and in England, took advantage of courses offered by the Canadian Khaki University, which was established late in 1918; these were designed to prepare an individual for the studies or an occupation which he would like to continue at home.

Athletes of the Canadian Corps

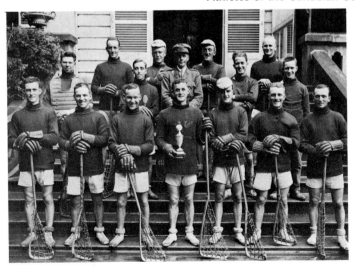

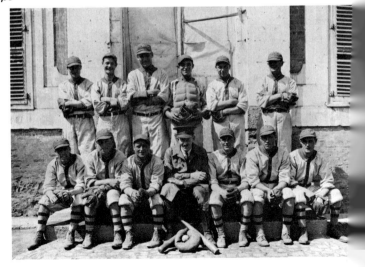

By February the return of other units of the Corps had already started via Britain for demobilization in Canada. This proceeded smoothly and expeditiously for the Corps, whose units remained together under their own officers, and thus, by orderly procedures the Canadian Corps passed into history. It was not the same with other Canadian units, where these precautions were not taken. The men, sick of waiting, rioted in various camps in England.

The rehabilitation of the men and women who had served in the First World War was of deep concern to the Government of Canada. In 1918 it set up a Department of Civil Re-establishment which has since become the Department of Veterans Affairs. Every soldier who had been overseas for six months (as well as everyone who had served in Canada for a year) received a gratuity based on his length of service and the rate of pay of his rank; single privates, for example, received payments which varied from $420 for three years' service or more to $210 for service of less than a year. Veterans who wished to farm were assisted with long-term loans and in this way more than 30,000 established themselves on farms. Others, who were disabled, received pensions which by the end of 1919 amounted to $22,500,000 annually for 91,000 veterans. Medical treatment continued, and there were opportunities for vocational training.

Rehabilitation

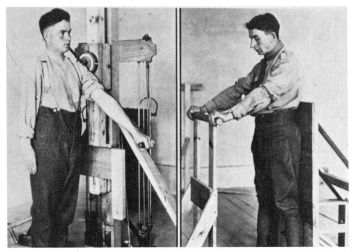

Treatment and rehabilitation

The task was enormous. The new department assumed responsibility for the welfare of the families of more than sixty thousand fatal casualties, as well as for the civil re-establishment of six hundred thousand men who had enlisted. Disabled veterans numbering 70,000 (of whom 196 were blind and 3500 had suffered amputation) required compensation, treatment and rehabilitation.

Veterans Affairs continues to administer hospitals and to ensure, in a thousand ways, fair treatment for those who served and survived, as well as the dignified commemoration of those who died. Its work is needed. Maimed and blinded men require something more than their own courage to help them live out their days.

Part Nine:
Canada's Other Soldiers

Courtesy of the National Gallery of Canada   *—Painted by Louis Keene*
CANADIANS OUTSIDE THE DEPOT, SIBERIA, RUSSIA

Not all Canada's soldiers served in the Canadian Corps.
Of 150,000 men on the Western Front when hostilities ceased
almost 40,000 were outside Currie's command and these men,
too, had a proud record. We have referred briefly to the Cavalry
Brigade of which much more could be written.

Canadian Railway Troops made an important contribution.
Early in the war, advancing troops found themselves miles
beyond their railheads and there were gaps which French
railway units vainly tried to close. It was natural that Canada
(where in the years shortly before the war more new railways
had been built than anywhere else in what was then the Empire)
should do the bulk of this. The first Canadian unit reached the

Railway work

Western Front at the middle of 1915 and from that time on the contribution grew steadily. Canadians were the first to construct light railways behind the firing line, and to use them for carrying troops, ammunition, and supplies to the trenches as well as for carrying wounded to the rear. From 1914 to the end of the war all light railway construction and maintenance on the British front was carried out by Canadian troops, often under fire; these men also fought as infantry, especially during the German offensives of 1918. From 1 April, 1917, to the end of the war the Corps of Canadian Railway Troops suffered 1,977 casualties.

Another major group consisted of Canadian Tunnelling Companies. Engineers, skilled in underground mining, were especially useful in siege warfare for tunnelling under the enemy's trenches to blow them up; or for cratering no-man's-land to provide advanced machine-gun positions in the attack. Three companies—the 1st, 2nd and 3rd—were eventually provided and these worked with British engineer units during most of the war. In 1918 Currie reorganized the Corps in preparation for open warfare and at that time the 1st and 2nd Tunnelling Companies were disbanded; their members (some 1,100 men) were distributed among the new engineer battalions which he formed. The value of this was proved by the speed with which the crossings of the Canal du Nord (on which the later victories at Bourlon and Cambrai depended to a large extent) were effected. The 3rd Tunnelling Company, however, remained as such until the end of the war.

A Canadian sawmill

122

Units of the Canadian Forestry Corps played a conspicuous part in the successful outcome of the war. British imports of lumber were seriously curtailed through submarine warfare; there was not enough for war requirements. Early in 1916 the 224th Forestry Battalion of nearly 1,600 men had crossed from Canada to work in Britain's woods, thus saving the limited merchant shipping for the carrying of munitions and food. Canadian foresters provided as much as 300,000 tons of sawn lumber and 5,000,000 tons of mining timber in one year's work. To save cross-Channel shipping, operations later spread to France and at the time of the Armistice there were 12,000 men of the Forestry Corps in France as well as almost 10,000 more in England.

All this was in the West, but Canadians served farther afield than that. Though Canada had no large bodies of troops in the Eastern Mediterranean theatre, five Canadian hospitals operated there during the Dardanelles campaign and for some time afterwards. The first to go were Nos. 1 and 3 Canadian Stationary Hospitals. They opened on the island of Lemnos

The King and H.M. Queen Mary visit the Canadian foresters

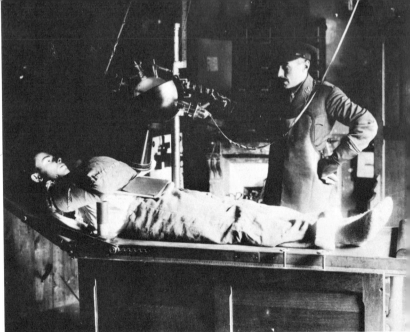

Hospitals in Salonika

during 1915 for the treatment of patients from Gallipoli.
After the failure of the Dardanelles venture, No. 1 moved to
Salonika and remained there until it returned to England in the
summer of 1917; No. 3 was transferred to France in April, 1916.
Two General Hospitals, No. 4 (University of Toronto) and No. 5,
were also in Salonika from the end of 1915 until the summer
of 1917. A fifth hospital (No. 5 Stationary), which became a
general hospital in the Middle East, spent several months
in Cairo.

Canada also sent a railway unit—the 1st Bridging Company
of 256 all ranks—to the Middle East where it assisted the
British against the Turks in Palestine. It helped to restore
railway communications between Jerusalem and Damascus
during the final victorious drive in 1918. And small parties of
Canadian Engineers operated barges on the Tigris and
Euphrates in Mesopotamia (now Iraq).

A kerosene shampoo for lice

124

The burial of Canadian nurses killed in a bombing raid in France

By far the largest contribution by Canada outside France and Flanders, however, was made in Russia where the Bolsheviks had withdrawn from the war. After the March Revolution of 1917, which overthrew the Czar, Russia technically was still a belligerent so that German troops remained on the Eastern Front. But the Bolsheviks changed all that, precipitately, and without consultation with Russia's allies. By their truce with Germany at the end of 1917 the Bolsheviks freed the Germans in the east so that divisions moved to the west.

The Bolsheviks were a minority, however, and there were many in Russia who were resolved to oppose them and to continue the war against Germany. Indeed, fighting had already broken out between a "Volunteer Army" and the Bolsheviks in the Don territory at the turn of the year. To assist these and other opponents of the Bolsheviks, and to help them re-create an Eastern Front, became the aim of Britain and France now that the German nightmare of war on two fronts was for all practical purposes over. This resolve hardened after the Bolsheviks signed the Treaty of Brest-Litovsk with Germany in March, 1918, for by that Germany had Russia in an iron grip. The resources of Russia lay wide open for German exploitation and these could be drawn upon to break the stranglehold of naval blockade. Nourished by these supplies, the enemy, it seemed, could prolong the war indefinitely. France and Britain, therefore, pushed forward plans for intervention with the dual purpose of re-creating an eastern front and of denying Russian supplies to the Germans.

Intervention eventually took place in three Russian theatres, south, north and east. In the south, Canada supplied forty officers and men to "Dunsterforce", largely British, which moved from Mesopotamia, through Persia, towards the Caucasus, Trans-Caspia, and Turkestan. Dunsterforce occupied the Caspian port of Baku in August 1918 and denied its oil to the Central Powers at a crucial time.

125

Bolshevik prisoners clearing the Archangel streets

In the north, Allied troops occupied the ports of Murmansk and Archangel in the summer of 1918 and prevented their use as German submarine bases against transatlantic convoys then busily engaged in conveying American troops to France. The 16th Brigade, Canadian Field Artillery, provided the artillery for the force in the Archangel area; ninety-two officers and N.C.O.s acted as instructors for anti-Bolshevik levies raised at Murmansk.

From October, 1918, onwards a much larger force—the Canadian Expeditionary Force, Siberia—about 4,000 strong, entered Vladivostok, in Eastern Russia. This was by far the most hopeful theatre, for a Czech Corps had already freed Siberia from Bolshevik control and was moving towards Moscow, beyond the Urals; furthermore, a Japanese contingent of 70,000 troops and an American one of 8,000 were also in Siberia. With the Armistice of 11 November, however, and the cessation of hostilities on the Western Front, there was no longer any purpose in creating an eastern front.

Nevertheless, anti-Bolshevik governments had grown up under Allied protection and it was British policy that these could not be abandoned to Bolshevik reprisals. Thus the interventionists, no matter how unwittingly, had become part of the Russian Civil War which had been fought between Whites and Reds for about a year. The policies of the Allies as to what to do about the Bolsheviks, however, differed widely. A private quarrel between America and Japan over the control of the Trans-Siberian Railway starved the White Russian forces on the Ural front of the munitions and supplies that they needed to maintain the struggle against the Bolsheviks. The Allies withdrew when the White cause no longer held any prospect of success.

Canadian gunners in North Russia

Public opinion in Canada, in any case, opposed any further participation in Russia by Canadian troops now that the war was over. The Canadian Expeditionary Force, which had taken no part in the fighting, left Vladivostok between April and June, 1919. Canadian troops at Archangel, who had fought the Bolsheviks relentlessly all winter and through the spring, also were withdrawn in June. Those in the Murmansk area stayed longer, but by September they, too, had left those distant shores.

The fighting in North Russia had taken place under the severest weather conditions ever experienced by Canadian troops. The hours of darkness, at times twenty out of twenty-four, were dispiriting enough as were the Arctic temperatures; to touch metal with the bare hand was like grasping red-hot iron and if a machine-gun jammed the only way of getting it going was by taking it apart and boiling it. Wounds in the open meant almost certain death. Fortunately Canadian casualties in North Russia had been light—eight killed and sixteen wounded.

Canadian troops in Vladivostok

Part Ten:
The Navy's Part

Courtesy of the National Gallery of Canada   *—Painted by Arthur Lismer*

MINESWEEPERS—HALIFAX

In 1914 the supremacy of Britain at sea had been recently
challenged by Germany. In 1897 Britain had fifty-four battleships
to Germany's fourteen. Britain's H.M.S. *Dreadnought*, which
appeared in 1905, made all older battleships obsolete. By 1914
both countries had built big-gun battleships of the Dreadnought
type and—though her lead had narrowed—Britain was still
ahead. She had twenty modern battleships; Germany had
thirteen comparable ships. The British lead was important for a

HMS Dreadnaught

country dependent on the use of the sea for food and the secure passage of ships carrying imports and exports for its industrial existence.

The main purpose of the Royal Navy, then, was to keep Britain's sea lines of communication open and to sever those of the enemy. Its ultimate purpose was blockade—to deny the enemy the resources needed to continue waging war. Blockade is a weapon slow to take effect but it had exerted a powerful influence on the final outcome before the war was over.

To frustrate this purpose, Germany must reduce Britain's naval strength and command of the seas. The German High Seas Fleet was not powerful enough to challenge the Grand Fleet, if it remained concentrated, but it might be possible to fall upon its separate parts and destroy it piecemeal. That was the genesis of the Battle of Jutland, fought on May 31, 1916, in the North Sea off the coast of Denmark.

The German plan to bring only part of the Grand Fleet to action miscarried; the High Seas Fleet of 100 ships of various types, manned by 45,000 officers and men, were to meet 148 ships and 60,000 officers and men before this naval battle— the biggest in history—was over.

Coastal patrol boat

HMCS Niobe

Aid for a torpedoed ship

131

Ships of the Battle Fleet at anchor in the Firth of Forth

The British suffered the greater losses in both ships and men. Three battle cruisers, three cruisers and eight torpedo boats were sunk against one battleship, one battle cruiser, four light cruisers and five torpedo boats on the German side. The Royal Navy lost 6;274 men in casualties against 2,545 in the German fleet. Ship for ship, the High Seas Fleet proved a match for the Royal Navy. Nevertheless the British were better able to afford the losses and the Grand Fleet continued to dominate the North Sea. After Jutland the High Seas Fleet remained in port, venturing out on only two occasions and those were brief. The Germans risked no more sea battles. Their shipyards ceased work on surface ships and switched to submarines. The British blockade of Germany went on.

After Jutland, Germany turned increasingly to submarine and mine warfare; the sinking of American vessels was a major factor in bringing the United States into the war. The ever-mounting toll of merchant vessels was critical for Britain, especially in the early months of 1917. In the summer of that year, however, the adoption of the convoy system caused sinkings to decline.

The Royal Canadian Navy's share in naval operations was small. At the outbreak of war there were only two ships— H.M.C.S. *Niobe,* a protected cruiser of 11,000 tons at Halifax, and a light cruiser, H.M.C.S. *Rainbow,* based on the West Coast at Esquimalt. Two submarines, acquired in the United States, were added to the naval defences at Esquimalt on 5 August. The control of these warships was handed over to the British Admiralty.

Ships of the Second Battle Cruiser Squadron which fought at Jutland

Nevertheless, the R.C.N. retained some responsibility for naval defence. This consisted in the main of providing part of the ship's companies of Canada's cruisers and submarines; setting up an Examination Service to check vessels entering Canadian ports; through the Naval Control Service, directing the movements of shipping; of the control of radio stations, afloat and ashore, through the Naval Control and Radio telegraph Services, which formed a vital link in the Admiralty's widespread intelligence system. From the very beginning the Admiralty deprecated the need for R.C.N. assistance, pointing out that warships could not be built quickly and that Canada's best contribution could be made on land. The increased tempo of submarine warfare and its spread into North American coastal waters caused the Admiralty to change its mind and at the end of 1916 Canada was asked to create a patrol force of thirty-six vessels for the forthcoming year.

The Canadian authorities attempted to comply. Vessels were obtained from other government departments, by charter, and by purchase from the United States; twelve anti-submarine trawlers were built in Canada. An officer from the Royal Navy came out to organize and command the patrols and the R.N. provided the trained crew members and the guns that Canada lacked. Newfoundland furnished five armed and manned vessels. Yet by the end of 1917, Canada was still short of the target of thirty-six ships.

Despite this inconspicuous beginning, in 1918 the Canadian Patrol Service was one of one hundred and twelve ships — under the command of Captain Walter Hose, a retired R.N.

officer who had served in the R.C.N. since 1911. To this total, the Royal Navy contributed twenty drifters, and their crews, while the United States Navy provided two torpedo boats and six submarine chasers. The United States also provided aircraft and pilots for a Royal Canadian Naval Air Service (which became operational in August 1918) until such time as Canada could provide her own. Flying boats escorted convoys in coastal waters and searched for submarines.

At the time of the Armistice the R.C.N. had grown to a force of more than a hundred war vessels and about 5,500 officers and men, a promising beginning for a future, and effective, navy. But this was not Canada's main contribution to the war at sea in the First World War. That lay in the provision of men, and of ships built in Canada, for the Royal Navy. Canada's first casualties of the war occurred at sea when four young midshipmen, serving in HMS *Good Hope,* lost their lives at the Battle of Coronel, fought off the west coast of Chile, on 1 November, 1914. Canada built more than sixty steel anti-submarine trawlers and a hundred wooden drifters; she assembled 550 anti-submarine motor launches in her yards. Additionally armed trawlers and coastal patrol motor boats were built for France. As for manpower, though there are no records of direct enlistments by Canadians into the Royal Navy it is known that the numbers were considerable.

One who tried to enlist in the Canadian services at the outbreak of the war was Rowland Richard Louis Bourke; he was rejected because of defective eyesight. Later, however, he was accepted into the Royal Naval Volunteer Reserve in England. On 10 May, 1918, Bourke, who was then a lieutenant commanding a motor-launch, followed H.M.S. *Vindictive* into Ostend during an attack on the port and rescued one officer and two of *Vindictive's* crew under heavy fire at close range. His launch was hit in fifty-five places, two of her crew killed and others wounded. Despite the damage, Bourke brought her out at reduced speed and turned the survivors over to a monitor which took his launch in tow. He won the V.C. for this exploit.

The numbers of those who were recruited by the R.C.N. for service with the R.N. are known: some 1,700 officers and men into the Overseas Division of the Royal Naval Canadian Volunteer Reserve; 264 officers into the Naval Service; 635 pilots for the Royal Naval Air Service; 107 surgeon-probationers; and 112 chief mechanics and mechanics for the Admiralty. These men, as well as a number of R.C.N. officers, served in many parts of the world.

Part Eleven:
The War in the Air

Courtesy of the National Gallery of Canada　　　*—Painted by C. R. W. Nevinson*

WAR IN THE AIR

Though Canada did not have an air force of her own in the First World War, Canadian airmen made an outstanding contribution. They served in the Royal Flying Corps and the Royal Naval Air Service—the British military and naval wings—and when the R.F.C. and R.N.A.S. were united to form the Royal Air Force on 1 April, 1918, more than 22,000 Canadians were in the R.A.F.

The first powered flight by a British subject in a heavier-than-air machine in the British Empire had been made in Canada. That was in 1909, on a chilly February day, when J. A. D. McCurdy soared briefly over the ice of Bras d'Or Lake at Baddeck Bay in the "Silver Dart". Canada thrilled to that achievement. But though test flights for military purposes were made at Petawawa in the summer of 1909, no steps were taken either for training or the purchase of aeroplanes before war broke out.

And yet, in August 1914, Colonel Hughes reversed his stand and sent a provisional "Canadian Aviation Corps", consisting of two officers, an N.C.O. and a Burgess-Dunne biplane purchased in the United States, to England. Its career was brief. One aviator returned to civil life in Canada almost immediately afterwards; the other was killed while making his first solo flight in England. The plane, which never flew, disappeared on Salisbury Plain and was believed to have been broken up for scrap.

Thereafter men who were interested in flying volunteered for the British service. Officers were seconded; men were discharged from the Canadian forces and re-enrolled as British airmen, either as cadets or for service as mechanics. Many cadets were enlisted by the British authorities in Canada and these had the same status as those enrolled in Britain. Through these channels 22,802 Canadians are known to have joined the British air services and many more also entered in other ways. They served as pilots, observers and mechanics in every theatre of the war. This impressive contribution spurred the Canadian authorities in 1918 to the conviction that Canada should have an air force of her own—essential to Canada's post-war military organization—which would not only be of use militarily but also as a training ground for commercial flying, in a country of vast distances, after the war. A start was made to create a small air force for overseas and a naval air service for home defence. Two purely Canadian squadrons were formed in England but neither became operational before the Armistice.

A start was made to form a Canadian air force in 1918—Nos. 1 and 2 Fighter Squadrons were formed but neither became operational before the Armistice

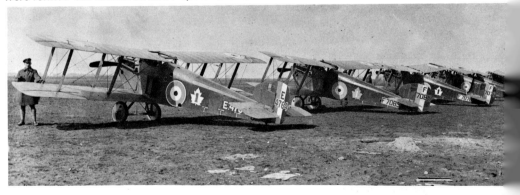

In static warfare, aerial reconnaissance was essential. Planes brought back photographs of the enemy's defences which were carefully studied before any attack; the Counter-Battery Office of the Canadian Corps, for example, found that more useful target information came from planes than any other source. Planes were also frequently used, especially in the final stages of the war, for bombing targets out of gun range. Not unnaturally, the enemy interfered with reconnaissance and bombing missions by using fighters; the swirling duels between opposing fighters ("dog fights"), each seeking to penetrate the other's guard, will always be associated with the air war of those years.

A sector of the Western Front from the air

Billy Bishop

Canadian airmen earned great distinction as fighter pilots. A man gaining five victories over enemy planes became an "ace" and of the top twenty-seven aces in the R.A.F., ten were Canadians. Each was credited with thirty or more victories. The third and fifth leading aces, among pilots of every nationality, Allied or enemy, were Canadians—Lieutenant-Colonel W. A. Bishop with seventy-two and Major Raymond Collishaw with sixty. Only Manfred von Richthofen (Germany) and Réné Fonck (France) bested Bishop, and only these and Ernst Udet (Germany) scored more than Collishaw.

Bishop, who gained about half his victories in French Nieuport Scouts, was the first Canadian airman to win the V.C. He did so on the morning of 2 June 1917, when he took off alone to shoot up a German aerodrome in the vicinity of Cambrai. Two enemy machines rose to meet the attack of the diving plane, and Bishop disposed of both. Two more enemy planes, rising simultaneously, closed on the single raider. One fell to the deadly fire of Bishop's gun and the other was driven off; out of ammunition, the Canadian returned to his home field.

Major W. G. Barker, formerly a machine-gunner in the 1st Canadian Mounted Rifles, won a second V.C. in a Sopwith Snipe, a British plane with a good all-round fighting performance. Since the end of April, 1917, the enemy had massed fighter formations into "circuses" and it was one of these that Barker encountered, alone, over Valenciennes on the morning of 27 October 1918. At this time the enemy had developed the 125-m.p.h. Fokker D VII biplane which combined speed and agility; it was an easily-handled plane with an exceptional rate of climb, able to "hang on to its propeller" and spray the underside of an opponent with bullets.

A group of airmen including Collishaw in naval uniform, France, July 1918

The burial of von Richthofen with an Australian firing party

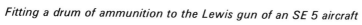

Fitting a drum of ammunition to the Lewis gun of an SE 5 aircraft

139

Loading photographic plates onto a DH 4 day Reconnaissance Bomber

Barker, flying high, shot down an enemy two-seater.
Then a D VII swooped up, wounding the Canadian with
accurate machine-gun fire. The Snipe dropped in a spinning
fall into the midst of fifteen Fokkers, three of which Barker
attacked; he accounted for at least one. In this action the
Canadian was again wounded. He lost consciousness briefly
but rallied to find himself the target of another formation at a
lower level. He sent one D VII down in flames but was himself
wounded for the third time. Then at 12,000 feet, he was
attacked by two more Fokkers, one of which he shot down at
less than ten feet. Barker crashed behind his own lines where he
recovered from his wounds.

This epic air-fight took place over an area where the
Canadian Corps was preparing for the Battle of Valenciennes.
Thousands of spellbound troops observed it, as well as a gunner
officer who described it well: "The spectacle of this attack
was the most magnificient encounter of any sort which I
have ever witnessed. The ancient performances of the
gladiators in the Roman arenas were far outclassed in the
epic character of the successive engagements in which enemy
machines, one after the other, were taken on and eliminated.
The spectators, in place of being restricted to the stone walls
of a Roman arena, had the horizon as their bounds and the
sky as their stage. The hoarse shout, or rather the prolonged
roar, which greeted the triumph of the British fighter, and
which echoed across the battlefront, was never matched in
Rome, nor do I think anywhere else or on any other occasion."

A crashed German aircraft outside a Zeppelin shed

Developing aerial photographs

Bombing up an Armstrong Whitworth FK 8

Canada's remaining air V.C. was won not by a fighter, but by the pilot of a less glamorous multi-purpose Armstrong-Whitworth F.K.8 two-seater aircraft. He was 2nd Lieutenant A. A. McLeod. On 27 March, 1918, at the time of the great German spring offensive in the region of the Somme, McLeod took off with an observer (Lieutenant A. W. Hammond) on a bombing and strafing mission near Albert. He was eighteen years old at the time.

Eight Fokker triplanes materialized and swept in to attack the heavier and slower machine. McLeod manoeuvred skilfully, enabling his observer to shoot down three triplanes, but a fourth set his plane on fire. The young pilot climbed out of the cockpit and onto the lower wing, leaning over to control the machine. He sideslipped to keep the flames on the other side while the observer continued to fire on the enemy until the ground was reached. Both McLeod and his observer were wounded several times but they kept up the unequal battle until the British aircraft finally crashed in no-man's-land. The plane was a blazing wreck, but, despite ground fire and a sixth wound from a bomb, McLeod dragged his companion to a place of safety. The observer subsequently recovered with the loss of a leg; McLeod died in hospital at Winnipeg later, the combined result of influenza and his wounds.

Canadian pilots also took part in the air defence of Great Britain. Ever since 1909 when a Frenchman, Louis Blériot, was the first man to fly the Channel in a heavier-than-air machine, Britain could no longer count on her surrounding waters for protection. The Germans, moreover, had Zeppelins and these lighter-than-air ships were capable of long flights.

The first aerial bombardment of the civilian population took place in January, 1915, when a Zeppelin raided Norfolk, in England. More frequent raids, especially on London, led to the formation of home defence squadrons, including No. 39, Royal Flying Corps, in April, 1916.

On the night of 1 October, 1916, Second Lieutenant W. J. Tempest, a Canadian pilot with this squadron, soared up from a grass-covered flying field in Essex in answer to an alert. Eleven Zeppelins had left bases on the North German coast during the afternoon, steered west in darkness, and one was known to be near London. Tempest pointed his slow B.E. 12 night-fighter towards the British capital.

Searchlights, wavering to and fro over London, at last converged on their quarry, holding the airship at the apex of a pyramid of light. Tempest saw this from fifteen miles away; he flew towards his target.

The air war over Britain

Though buffeted by bursting anti-aircraft shells, the Canadian managed to get through them unscathed. His aircraft, clearly recognizable in the searchlight illumination and from its exhaust flames, was sighted by the Zeppelin which then salvoed her bombs and sheered off to the north, climbing rapidly. Tempest, now free of anti-aircraft bursts, dived at the airship, firing his Lewis gun as he did so; he banked, and then fired burst after burst of explosive and incendiary bullets into her underside. "I noticed her begin to go red inside like an enormous Chinese lantern," Tempest wrote. "She then shot up about two hundred feet, paused, and came roaring down straight on to me before I had time to get out of the way. I nosedived for all I was worth, with the Zepp tearing after me, and expected every minute to be engulfed in the flames. I put my machine into a spin and just managed to corkscrew out of the way as she shot past me, roaring like a furnace."

Canadian officers of the Royal Naval Air Service, stationed on the east coast of England, also shot down airships. They were Lieutenant S. D. Culley, Lieutenant B. D. Hobbs, and Major R. Leckie who was credited with two. Culley's feat was perhaps the most spectacular. His Camel took off at sea from the deck of a towed lighter, rose, and sent a Zeppelin plunging seawards in a blazing mass.

Deeds such as these account for the high reputation which Canadians enjoyed in the Royal Air Force of whose officers almost a quarter came from Canada. Their contribution was important in the war, and was of great benefit to the future of Canada in the air as well. Of greater importance, perhaps, was the training or airmen which took place in Canada during the last two years of the war. Because of the heavy losses experienced by the Royal Flying Corps at the Battles of the Somme, increased facilities for flying training became imperative. Canada was chosen as the site for this and the advance party of an R.F.C. training brigade arrived there in 1917. Shortly afterwards the first of six large flying stations opened at Camp Borden where training began in Curtiss JN-4 aircraft. Over 1,300 Curtiss Jennies were produced by Canadian Aeroplanes Limited of Toronto, to meet the training requirements of the R.F.C. and R.A.F. in Canada, and this was of great importance to the development of the country when the war was over.

Immense strides, technologically, took place under the stimulus of war. In 1919, only ten years after the first flight of the "Silver Dart", for example, the Atlantic was spanned by Alcock and Brown in a converted Vickers Vimy bomber. Canada kept abreast of these developments and this was of value to the R.C.A.F. and the progress of civil aviation in the post-war years.

*Sopwith Camels of
No. 45 Squadron RFC*

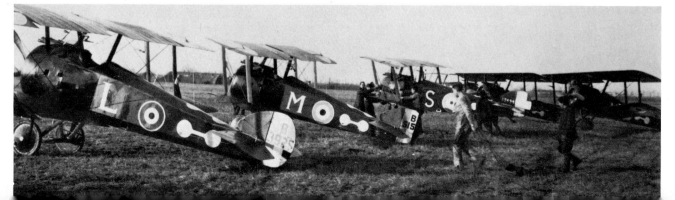

Part Twelve:
Conclusion

Courtesy of the Department of National Defence

NATIONAL WAR MEMORIAL, OTTAWA

The war was over and the nations took stock. Among them they had lost eight million lives and more than that if we consider those civilians who disappeared as the conflict swept over vast areas of the world. Twenty-one million more had been wounded and of these a large number were so badly gassed or maimed that they would be invalids for life.

The Canadians cross the Rhine

146

147

The Victory Parade in London

We have seen something of what Canada had done by land, sea and air, especially through the Canadian Corps, "the greatest national achievement of the Canadian people since the Dominion came into being." From amateur beginnings the Corps had become more than a match for the highly professional Germans and ever since the Somme its record had been one of unbroken victory. It ended the war as a superb fighting machine that earned for its country a reputation second to none in the Allied armies.

What had all this cost? It is estimated that about 10,000 Canadians served in the navy and 24,000 in the air forces; 619,636 Canadian men and women served with the army. Of those in all services 60,661 did not return, roughly ten per cent of all who enlisted. Most of these were soldiers—59,544—as were those who were wounded: 172,950 from the army.

Currie stands behind the King while Canadians march past—Winston Churchill and the Army commanders are in the foreground

Borden addresses troops awaiting embarkation in England

Preparing soldiers' documents prior to demobilization

Leaving Liverpool for Canada

That such a war record would carry Canada to full autonomy had been foreseen by Sir Robert Borden, and so it proved. Canada's unstinted war effort, and Borden's tactics, paid off. In March, 1917, Borden attended the first meeting of the Imperial War Cabinet at the invitation of the British; he had protested that British statesmen were taking upon themselves the framing of war policy without bothering to consult the Dominions. At these meetings Borden noted with satisfaction that "Great Britain presided but the Dominions met her on equal terms"; it was, as we have seen, Borden's own resolution that substituted the name "Commonwealth" for "Empire" after he had called for the Dominions to be recognized as antonomous nations within the Commonwealth.

The Olympic *with returned soldiers, a painting by Arthur Lismer*

Courtesy of the National Gallery of Canada

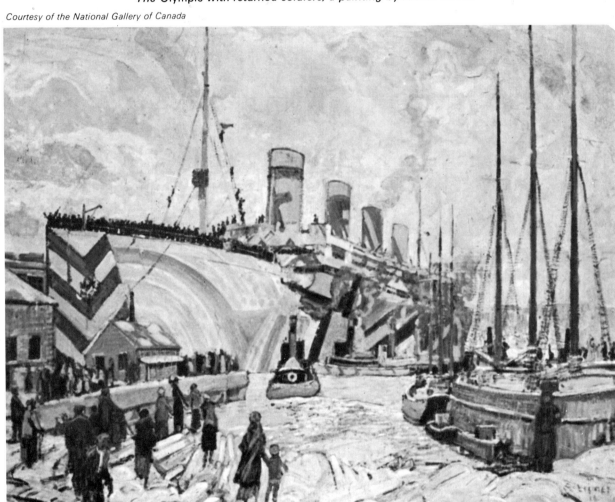

"Well, if you knows of a better 'ole, go to it"

"Please let us know, as soon as possible, the number of tins of raspberry jam issued to you last Friday"

Bairnsfather's cartoons were popular with Canadian troops

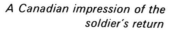

A Canadian impression of the soldier's return

Funeral of the French wife of a Canadian soldier

154

Canada, The Great Provider

155

A creditable war effort would constitute a charter of full nationhood and at the end of the war it was obvious that Canada's war effort had been more than creditable. After the Armistice, Borden opposed the return of Canadian troops from Siberia (which Canadian public opinion demanded) because Canada's *"position"* and *"prestige"* would be impaired. Because of her position and prestige, largely earned by the magnificient Canadian Corps, Canada signed the Peace Treaties separately and was seated separately at the League of Nations. There is no doubt, with that, that the status of nationhood had been achieved.

The sacrifices of the men and women who served so bravely in the First World War fulfilled a national purpose.

Almost one in ten Canadians did not return

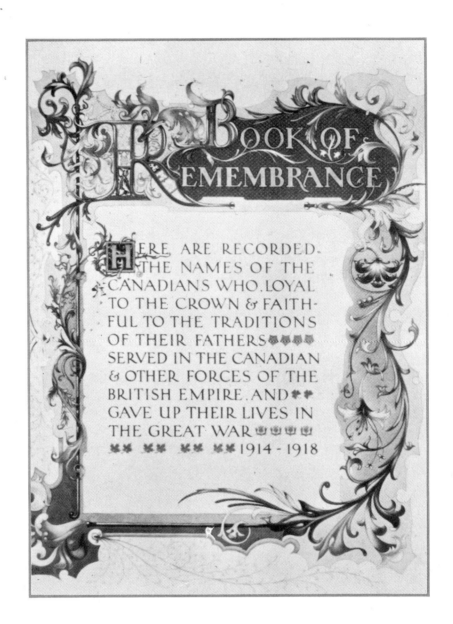

THE BOOK OF REMEMBRANCE

HERE ARE RECORDED THE NAMES OF THE CANADIANS WHO, LOYAL TO THE CROWN & FAITHFUL TO THE TRADITIONS OF THEIR FATHERS SERVED IN THE CANADIAN & OTHER FORCES OF THE BRITISH EMPIRE, AND GAVE UP THEIR LIVES IN THE GREAT WAR 1914 - 1918

158

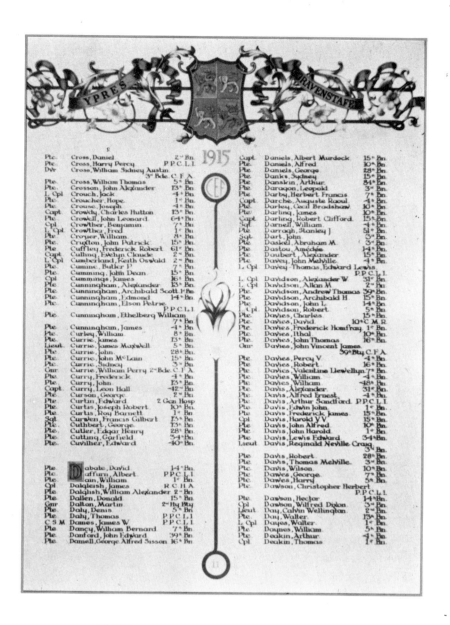

YPRES — GRAVENSTAFEL

1915

Pte.	Cross, Daniel	2ⁿᵈ Bn.	Capt.	Daniels, Albert Murdock	15ᵗʰ Bn.
Pte.	Cross, Harry Percy	P.P.C.L.I.	Pte.	Daniels, Alfred	10ᵗʰ Bn.
Dvr.	Cross, William Sidney Austin		Pte.	Daniels, George	28ᵗʰ Bn.
		3ʳᵈ Bde. C.F.A.	Pte.	Danks, Sydney	15ᵗʰ Bn.
Pte.	Cross, William Thomas	5ᵗʰ Bn.	Pte.	Danskin, Arthur	84ᵗʰ Bn.
Pte.	Crossan, John Alexander	13ᵗʰ Bn.	Pte.	Daragon, Leopold	3ʳᵈ Bn.
L.Cpl.	Crouch, Jack	4ᵗʰ Bn.	Pte.	Darby, Herbert Francis	7ᵗʰ Bn.
Pte.	Croucher, Hope	1ˢᵗ Bn.	Capt.	Darche, Auguste Raoul	4ᵗʰ Bn.
Pte.	Crouse, Joseph	4ᵗʰ Bn.	Pte.	Darley, Cecil Bradshaw	10ᵗʰ Bn.
Capt.	Crowdy, Charles Hutton	13ᵗʰ Bn.	Pte.	Darling, James	10ᵗʰ Bn.
Pte.	Crowell, John Leonard	64ᵗʰ Bn.	Capt.	Darling, Robert Clifford	15ᵗʰ Bn.
Cpl.	Crowther, Benjamin	7ᵗʰ Bn.	Sgt.	Darnell, William	4ᵗʰ Bn.
L.Cpl.	Crowther, Fred	1ˢᵗ Bn.	Pte.	Darragh, Stanley J	5ᵗʰ Bn.
Pte.	Croyer, William	8ᵗʰ Bn.	Sgt.	Dart, John	5ᵗʰ Bn.
Pte.	Cruxton, John Patrick	15ᵗʰ Bn.	Pte.	Daskel, Abraham M	3ʳᵈ Bn.
Pte.	Cuffley, Frederick Robert	61ˢᵗ Bn.	Pte.	Dastou, Amédée	14ᵗʰ Bn.
Capt.	Culling, Evelyn Claude	2ⁿᵈ Bn.	Pte.	Doubert, Alexander	15ᵗʰ Bn.
L.Cpl.	Cumberland, Keith Oswald	2ⁿᵈ Bn.	Pte.	Davey, John Melville	4ᵗʰ Bn.
Pte.	Cumine, Butler P	7ᵗʰ Bn.	L.Cpl.	Davey-Thomas, Edward Lewis	
Pte.	Cumming, John Dean	15ᵗʰ Bn.			P.P.C.L.I.
Cpl.	Cummings, James	16ᵗʰ Bn.	L.Cpl.	Davidson, Alexander W	31ˢᵗ Bn.
Pte.	Cunningham, Alexander	13ᵗʰ Bn.	L.Cpl.	Davidson, Allan M	2ⁿᵈ Bn.
Pte.	Cunningham, Archibald Scott	1ˢᵗ Bn.	Pte.	Davidson, Andrew Thomas	59ᵗʰ Bn.
Pte.	Cunningham, Edmond	14ᵗʰ Bn.	Pte.	Davidson, Archibald H	15ᵗʰ Bn.
Pte.	Cunningham, Elson Petrie		Pte.	Davidson, John L	14ᵗʰ Bn.
		P.P.C.L.I.	L.Cpl.	Davidson, Robert	5ᵗʰ Bn.
Pte.	Cunningham, Ethelberg William		Pte.	Davies, Charles	15ᵗʰ Bn.
		7ᵗʰ Bn.	Pte.	Davies, David	10ᵗʰ C.M.R.
Pte.	Cunningham, James	4ᵗʰ Bn.	Pte.	Davies, Frederick Homfray	1ˢᵗ Bn.
Pte.	Currey, William	8ᵗʰ Bn.	Pte.	Davies, Ithal	10ᵗʰ Bn.
Pte.	Currie, James	13ᵗʰ Bn.	Pte.	Davies, John Thomas	16ᵗʰ Bn.
Lieut.	Currie, James Maxwell	5ᵗʰ Bn.	Gnr.	Davies, John Vincent James	
Pte.	Currie, John	28ᵗʰ Bn.			59ᵗʰ Bty. C.F.A.
Pte.	Currie, John McLean	15ᵗʰ Bn.	Pte.	Davies, Percy V	16ᵗʰ Bn.
Pte.	Currie, Sidney	5ᵗʰ Bn.	Pte.	Davies, Robert	16ᵗʰ Bn.
Gnr.	Currie, William Perry	2ⁿᵈ Bde. C.F.A.	Pte.	Davies, Valentine Llewellyn	7ᵗʰ Bn.
Pte.	Curry, Frederick	4ᵗʰ Bn.	Pte.	Davies, William	4ᵗʰ Bn.
Pte.	Curry, John	13ᵗʰ Bn.	Pte.	Davies, William	48ᵗʰ Bn.
Capt.	Curry, Leon Hall	42ⁿᵈ Bn.	Pte.	Davis, Alexander	31ˢᵗ Bn.
Pte.	Curson, George	2ⁿᵈ Bn.	Pte.	Davis, Alfred Ernest	4ᵗʰ Bn.
Pte.	Curtin, Edward	2 Gen. Hosp.	Pte.	Davis, Arthur Sandford	P.P.C.L.I.
Pte.	Curtis, Joseph Robert	10ᵗʰ Bn.	Pte.	Davis, Edwin John	1ˢᵗ Bn.
Pte.	Curtis, Roy Barnett	1ˢᵗ Bn.	Pte.	Davis, Frederick James	15ᵗʰ Bn.
Sgt.	Curven, Francis Gilbert	15ᵗʰ Bn.	Cpl.	Davis, Harold Y V	15ᵗʰ Bn.
Pte.	Cuthbert, George	13ᵗʰ Bn.	Pte.	Davis, John Alfred	10ᵗʰ Bn.
Pte.	Cutler, Edgar Henry	28ᵗʰ Bn.	Pte.	Davis, John Harold	1ˢᵗ Bn.
Pte.	Cutting, Garfield	54ᵗʰ Bn.	Pte.	Davis, Lewis Edward	54ᵗʰ Bn.
Pte.	Cuvilher, Edward	40ᵗʰ Bn.	Lieut.	Davis, Reginald Neville Craig	
					5ᵗʰ Bn.
			Pte.	Davis, Robert	28ᵗʰ Bn.
			Pte.	Davis, Thomas Melville	3ʳᵈ Bn.
Pte.	Dabate, David	14ᵗʰ Bn.	Pte.	Davis, Wilson	10ᵗʰ Bn.
Pte.	Daffurn, Albert	P.P.C.L.I.	Pte.	Dawes, George	7ᵗʰ Bn.
Pte.	Dain, William	1ˢᵗ Bn.	Pte.	Dawes, Harry	5ᵗʰ Bn.
Cpl.	Dalgleish, James	R.C.H.A.	Pte.	Dawson, Christopher Herbert	
Pte.	Dalglish, William Alexander	2ⁿᵈ Bn.			P.P.C.L.I.
Pte.	Dallen, Donald	15ᵗʰ Bn.	Pte.	Dawson, Hector	14ᵗʰ Bn.
Gnr.	Dalton, Martin	2ⁿᵈ Hy. Bty.	Cpl.	Dawson, Wilfred Dixon	3ʳᵈ Bn.
Pte.	Daly, Denis	5ᵗʰ Bn.	Lieut.	Day, Calvin Wellington	2ⁿᵈ Bn.
Pte.	Daly, Thomas	P.P.C.L.I.	Pte.	Day, Walter	13ᵗʰ Bn.
C.S.M.	Dames, James W	P.P.C.L.I.	L.Cpl.	Dayes, Walter	1ˢᵗ Bn.
Pte.	Dancy, William Bernard	7ᵗʰ Bn.	Pte.	Daynes, William	5ᵗʰ Bn.
Pte.	Danford, John Edward	59ᵗʰ Bn.	Pte.	Deakin, Arthur	4ᵗʰ Bn.
Pte.	Darnell, George Alfred Sisson	16ᵗʰ Bn.	Cpl.	Deakin, Thomas	1ˢᵗ Bn.

THEY ARE TOO NEAR TO BE GREAT
BUT OUR CHILDREN SHALL
UNDERSTAND WHEN AND HOW
OUR FATE WAS CHANGED
AND BY WHOSE HAND.

Index